# First World War
### and Army of Occupation
# War Diary
### France, Belgium and Germany

29 DIVISION
Divisional Troops
497 (1/3 Kent) Field Company Royal Engineers
2 October 1915 - 27 October 1919

WO95/2293/2

The Naval & Military Press Ltd
www.nmarchive.com
**Published in association with The National Archives**

Published by

## The Naval & Military Press Ltd

Unit 10 Ridgewood Industrial Park,

Uckfield, East Sussex,

TN22 5QE England

Tel: +44 (0) 1825 749494

www.naval-military-press.com

www.nmarchive.com

*This diary has been reprinted in facsimile from the original. Any imperfections are inevitably reproduced and the quality may fall short of modern type and cartographic standards.*

**© Crown Copyright**
**Images reproduced by permission of The National Archives, London, England, 2015.**

# Contents

| Document type | Place/Title | Date From | Date To |
|---|---|---|---|
| Heading | WO95/2293/2 497 (1/3 Kent) Field Company Royal Engineers | | |
| Heading | 29th Division Divl Engineers 1-3rd (kent) Fld Coy R.E. Mar 1916 497th (Kent) Fld Coy R.E. Mar 1916-Oct 1919 From Dardanelles 52 Div Troops | | |
| Heading | 29th Divisional Engineers Arrived Marseilles From Egypt 22.3.16 1/3rd Kent Field Company R.E. March 1916 | | |
| Miscellaneous | 1/3 Kent Fd Coy R.E. Vol I BEF From MEF | | |
| War Diary | Suez | 01/03/1916 | 11/03/1916 |
| War Diary | Suez Camp | 12/03/1916 | 14/03/1916 |
| War Diary | Hmt Alaunia | 15/03/1916 | 22/03/1916 |
| War Diary | Marseilles | 22/03/1916 | 22/03/1916 |
| War Diary | In Train | 23/03/1916 | 25/03/1916 |
| War Diary | Monflieres | 25/03/1916 | 30/03/1916 |
| War Diary | Surcamp | 30/03/1916 | 31/03/1916 |
| War Diary | Beauval | 31/03/1916 | 31/03/1916 |
| Heading | 29th Divisional Engineers 1/3rd Kent Field Company R.E. April 1916 | | |
| Miscellaneous | 1/3rd Kent Fd Coy R.E. Vol II | | |
| War Diary | Beauval | 01/04/1916 | 05/04/1916 |
| War Diary | Englebelmer | 06/04/1916 | 30/04/1916 |
| Miscellaneous | Appendix No 1 | | |
| Miscellaneous | Bangalore Torpedo Appendix No 2 | | |
| Miscellaneous | Appendix Vol I 1/3 Kent Fd Coy R.E | | |
| Miscellaneous | O.C. 1/3rd Kent Field Coy R.E. | 11/04/1916 | 11/04/1916 |
| Operation(al) Order(s) | 28th Brigade Operation Order No 44 | 02/04/1916 | 02/04/1916 |
| Miscellaneous | March Table "A" | | |
| Heading | 29th Divisional Engineers 1/3rd Kent Field Company R.E. May 1916 | | |
| War Diary | Englebelmer | 01/05/1916 | 31/05/1916 |
| Heading | 29th Divisional Engineers 1/3rd Kent Field Company R.E. June 1916 | | |
| War Diary | Englebelmer | 01/06/1916 | 24/06/1916 |
| War Diary | Bivouacs | 25/06/1916 | 28/06/1916 |
| War Diary | Englebelmer Bivouacs | 29/06/1916 | 30/06/1916 |
| Heading | 25th Divisional Engineers 1/3rd Kent Field Company R.E. July 1916 | | |
| Heading | War Diary of 1/3rd Kent Field Company R.E. (T.F) from 1st to 31st July 1916 Volume X | | |
| War Diary | Englebemer Bivouacs | 01/07/1916 | 01/07/1916 |
| War Diary | Front Trenches | 02/07/1916 | 03/07/1916 |
| War Diary | Englebelmer | 03/07/1916 | 26/07/1916 |
| War Diary | Louvencourt | 26/07/1916 | 31/07/1916 |
| Heading | 29th Divisional Engineers 1/3rd Kent Field Company RE. August 1916 | | |
| War Diary | H.7.a.2.9 | 01/08/1916 | 31/08/1916 |
| Heading | 29th Divisional Engineers 1/3rd Kent Field Company R.E. September 1916 | | |
| War Diary | H.7 A.2.9 | 01/09/1916 | 30/09/1916 |

| | | | |
|---|---|---|---|
| Heading | 29th Divisional Engineers 1/3rd Kent Field Company R.E. October 1916 | | |
| War Diary | H7a29 | 01/10/1916 | 01/10/1916 |
| War Diary | Bradhoek | 02/10/1915 | 05/10/1915 |
| War Diary | Houtkerque | 05/10/1916 | 05/10/1916 |
| War Diary | Bradhoek | 04/10/1916 | 04/10/1916 |
| War Diary | Houtkerque | 06/10/1916 | 06/10/1916 |
| War Diary | Enroute | 07/10/1916 | 08/10/1916 |
| War Diary | Allonville | 09/10/1916 | 10/10/1916 |
| War Diary | Buire | 10/10/1916 | 13/10/1916 |
| War Diary | Mametz Wood | 14/10/1916 | 20/10/1916 |
| War Diary | Bernafay Wood Camp | 20/10/1916 | 24/10/1916 |
| War Diary | S 23 a 48 | 24/10/1916 | 27/10/1916 |
| War Diary | S 23 a 48 | 28/10/1916 | 30/10/1916 |
| War Diary | S28 Cent | 30/10/1916 | 31/10/1916 |
| Operation(al) Order(s) | C.R.E's. Order No 23 | 29/10/1916 | 29/10/1916 |
| Miscellaneous | Movement of Field Companies. | | |
| Heading | 29th Division 1/3rd Kent Field Company R.E. November 1916 | | |
| War Diary | S26 Cent Corbie | 01/11/1916 | 11/11/1916 |
| War Diary | Meaulte | 12/11/1916 | 12/11/1916 |
| War Diary | Sandpits Camp E24 a Cent | 13/11/1916 | 13/11/1916 |
| War Diary | Sandpits Camp | 14/11/1916 | 17/11/1916 |
| War Diary | Bernafay Wood S 29 c 32 | 17/11/1916 | 30/11/1916 |
| Heading | 29th Divisional Engineers 1/3rd Kent Field Company R.E. December 1916 | | |
| Heading | War Diary of 1/3rd Kent Field Coy R.E. (T) from December 1st 1916 To December 31st 1916 (Volume 1) | | |
| War Diary | Bernafay Wood S.29.c.32 | 01/12/1916 | 11/12/1916 |
| War Diary | Mansel Camp | 11/12/1916 | 12/12/1916 |
| War Diary | Meaulte | 13/12/1916 | 13/12/1916 |
| War Diary | Pecquigny & Corbie | 14/12/1916 | 14/12/1916 |
| War Diary | Pecquigny | 15/12/1916 | 31/12/1916 |
| Heading | War Diary of 1/3rd Kent Field Co., R.E. for Month Of January 1917 Volume XVI | | |
| War Diary | Picquigny | 01/01/1917 | 09/01/1917 |
| War Diary | Daours | 10/01/1917 | 15/01/1917 |
| War Diary | Meaulte | 16/01/1917 | 26/01/1917 |
| War Diary | S 29 C 32 Bernafay Wood | 27/01/1917 | 31/01/1917 |
| Heading | War Diary 497th (Kent) Field Co. R.E. February 1st To February 28th 1917 Volume XVII | | |
| War Diary | Bernafay Wood | 01/02/1917 | 06/02/1917 |
| War Diary | Heilly | 07/02/1917 | 20/02/1917 |
| War Diary | Mansel Camp | 21/02/1917 | 21/02/1917 |
| War Diary | Combles | 21/02/1917 | 28/02/1917 |
| Heading | War Diary of 497th (Kent) Field Co. R.E. From 1st March, 1917 To 31st March, 1917 (Volume XVIII) | | |
| War Diary | Combles | 01/03/1917 | 10/03/1917 |
| War Diary | Heilly | 12/03/1917 | 19/03/1917 |
| War Diary | Saisseval | 20/03/1917 | 30/03/1917 |
| War Diary | Pernoise | 31/03/1917 | 31/03/1917 |
| Heading | War Diary of 497th (Kent) Field Co. R.E. From 1st April, 1917 To 30th April, 1917 Volume XIX | | |
| War Diary | Pernoise | 01/04/1917 | 01/04/1917 |
| War Diary | Gezaincourt | 01/04/1917 | 02/04/1917 |
| War Diary | Pommera | 02/04/1917 | 05/04/1917 |

| | | | |
|---|---|---|---|
| War Diary | Oppy | 05/04/1917 | 06/04/1917 |
| War Diary | Warluzel | 07/04/1917 | 07/04/1917 |
| War Diary | Humbercamps | 08/04/1917 | 11/04/1917 |
| War Diary | Simencourt | 11/04/1917 | 12/04/1917 |
| War Diary | Arras | 13/04/1917 | 25/04/1917 |
| War Diary | Berneville | 25/04/1917 | 26/04/1917 |
| War Diary | Wanquetin | 26/04/1917 | 26/04/1917 |
| War Diary | Fonquevillers | 27/04/1917 | 30/04/1917 |
| Heading | War Diary of 497th (Kent) Field Co. R.E. From 1st May, 1917 To 31st May, 1917 Volume XX | | |
| War Diary | Fonquevillers Gouy-En-Artois | 01/05/1917 | 02/05/1917 |
| War Diary | Arras | 02/05/1917 | 07/05/1917 |
| War Diary | Dainville | 08/05/1917 | 14/05/1917 |
| War Diary | In Front of Arras At H32 a 8.2 | 15/05/1917 | 20/05/1917 |
| War Diary | H32a82 | 21/05/1917 | 31/05/1917 |
| Heading | War Diary of 497th (Kent) Field Co. R.E. From 1st June, 1917 To 30th June, 1917 Volume XXI | | |
| War Diary | Mt. Tilloy H32 A82 | 01/06/1917 | 02/06/1917 |
| War Diary | Berneville | 02/06/1917 | 02/06/1917 |
| War Diary | Gorges | 03/06/1917 | 26/06/1917 |
| War Diary | Proven | 27/06/1917 | 27/06/1917 |
| War Diary | C19c16 | 28/06/1917 | 30/06/1917 |
| Heading | War Diary of 497th (Kent) Field Company R.E. From 1st July, 1917 To 30th July, 1917 Volume XXII | | |
| War Diary | C19c.1.6 | 01/07/1917 | 08/07/1917 |
| War Diary | Sheet 28 C 19 c.1.6 | 09/07/1917 | 20/07/1917 |
| War Diary | Proven | 21/07/1917 | 31/07/1917 |
| Heading | War Diary of 497th (Kent) Field Co. R.E. From 1st August, 1917. To 31st August 1917 Volume XXIII | | |
| War Diary | Proven | 01/08/1917 | 06/08/1917 |
| War Diary | Lunaville Farm | 07/08/1917 | 25/08/1917 |
| War Diary | Portsdown Camp Proven | 26/08/1917 | 31/08/1917 |
| War Diary | Portsdown Camp Proven | 01/09/1917 | 19/09/1917 |
| War Diary | Elverdinghe | 20/09/1917 | 30/09/1917 |
| Heading | War Diary of 497th Kent Field Company R.E. From 1st September, 1917 To 30th September, 1917. Volume XXIV | | |
| Heading | War Diary of 497th (Kent) Field Company R.E. From 1st October, 1917, To 31st October 1917 Volume XXV | | |
| War Diary | Elverdinghe | 01/10/1917 | 09/10/1917 |
| War Diary | Proven | 10/10/1917 | 16/10/1917 |
| War Diary | Hopoutre | 16/10/1917 | 16/10/1917 |
| War Diary | Beaumetz Riviere | 17/10/1917 | 17/10/1917 |
| War Diary | Blaireville | 18/10/1917 | 19/10/1917 |
| War Diary | Blaireville | 20/10/1917 | 21/10/1917 |
| War Diary | Courcelles | 22/10/1917 | 25/10/1917 |
| War Diary | Neuchcourt | 26/10/1917 | 26/10/1917 |
| War Diary | W.5.b | 27/10/1917 | 31/10/1917 |
| Heading | War Diary of 497th (Kent) Field Coy. R.E. Volume 26 (November 1917) | | |
| War Diary | W 5 b Gouzeancourt | 01/11/1917 | 03/11/1917 |
| War Diary | Sorel Le Grand | 03/11/1917 | 18/11/1917 |
| War Diary | Georgement | 20/11/1917 | 26/11/1917 |
| War Diary | Rem H.Q R.8.b.9.5 | 27/11/1917 | 30/11/1917 |
| Heading | War Diary of 497th (Kent) Fd Co R.E 1/12/17 To 31/12/17 Volume XXVII | | |

| | | | |
|---|---|---|---|
| War Diary | Huclier | 01/12/1917 | 01/12/1917 |
| War Diary | Sorel Le Grand | 02/12/1917 | 06/12/1917 |
| War Diary | Berlencourt | 07/12/1917 | 16/12/1917 |
| War Diary | Aubrometz | 17/12/1917 | 17/12/1917 |
| War Diary | Bealencourt | 18/12/1917 | 18/12/1917 |
| War Diary | Gournay | 19/12/1917 | 31/12/1917 |
| Heading | War Diary of 497th (Kent) Field Coy R.E. From 1st January 1918 To 31st January 1918 Volume XXVIII | | |
| War Diary | Gourney | 01/01/1918 | 03/01/1918 |
| War Diary | Wizernes | 03/01/1918 | 16/01/1918 |
| War Diary | Ypres | 17/01/1918 | 31/01/1918 |
| Heading | War Diary of 497th (Kent) Field Coy R.E. From 1/2/18 To 28/2/18 | | |
| War Diary | Ypres | 01/02/1918 | 28/02/1918 |
| War Diary | War Diary of 497th (Kent) Field Coy. R.E. From 1/3/18 To 31/3/18 Volume No 30 | | |
| War Diary | Ypres | 01/03/1918 | 31/03/1918 |
| Heading | 29th Divisional Engineers 497th (Kent) Field Company R.E. April 1918 | | |
| Heading | War Diary of 497th (Kent) Fd Coy R.E. From 1/4/18 To 30/4/18 Volume No 26 | | |
| War Diary | Wieltje Dug Outs | 01/04/1918 | 09/04/1918 |
| War Diary | St. Jan Ter Biezen | 10/04/1918 | 11/04/1918 |
| War Diary | Near Bailleul | 12/04/1918 | 15/04/1918 |
| War Diary | Boeschepe | 15/04/1918 | 17/04/1918 |
| War Diary | Abeele | 18/04/1918 | 21/04/1918 |
| War Diary | Nr Hondeghem | 22/04/1918 | 27/04/1918 |
| War Diary | Au Souverain | 28/04/1918 | 30/04/1918 |
| Heading | War Diary 497th (Kent) Field Coy RE From 1/5/18 To 31/5/18 Volume No. 32 | | |
| War Diary | Au Souverain | 01/05/1918 | 31/05/1918 |
| Heading | War Diary of 497th (Kent) Field Co RE From 1-6-18 To 30-6-18 Volume No 33 | | |
| War Diary | Dismounted Position of Coy F/U Souverain Mountialportion Of Company D.7.b.1.9 | 01/06/1918 | 21/06/1918 |
| War Diary | EEK Hout Casteel C.6.c.1.5 | 22/06/1918 | 24/06/1918 |
| War Diary | EEK Hout Casteel | 25/06/1918 | 30/06/1918 |
| Heading | War Diary of 497th (Kent) Field Co RE From 1-7-18 To 31-7-18 Volume No 34 | | |
| War Diary | EEK Hout Casteel (C.6.c.75.) | 01/07/1918 | 15/07/1918 |
| War Diary | Bandringhem (A.18.c.1.5) | 16/07/1918 | 23/07/1918 |
| War Diary | Bavinchove (O.16.a.6.5) | 23/07/1918 | 31/07/1918 |
| Heading | War Diary of 497th Field Coy RE (T) From 1/8/18 To 31/8/18 Volume No 35 | | |
| War Diary | Bavinchove C.16.a.6.5 | 01/08/1918 | 02/08/1918 |
| War Diary | 27/W.13.b.5.5 | 03/08/1918 | 23/08/1918 |
| War Diary | Klite Hill 27/W.23.a.64 | 24/08/1918 | 31/08/1918 |
| Heading | War Diary of 497th Field Coy RE From 1/9/18 To 30/9/18 Volume No. XXXVI | | |
| War Diary | Klite Hill 27/W.23.a.6.4 | 01/09/1918 | 01/09/1918 |
| War Diary | X.21.d.5.8 | 02/09/1918 | 02/09/1918 |
| War Diary | A.2.d.5.8 | 03/09/1918 | 04/09/1918 |
| War Diary | A.6.d.4.6 | 05/09/1918 | 09/09/1918 |
| War Diary | 27/X19.a.0.6 | 10/09/1918 | 11/09/1918 |
| War Diary | Hazebrouck | 12/09/1918 | 18/09/1918 |
| War Diary | 28/A.30.d.0.6 | 19/09/1918 | 20/09/1918 |

| Type | Description | Start | End |
|---|---|---|---|
| War Diary | A.30.c.7.1 | 22/09/1918 | 27/09/1918 |
| War Diary | Infantry Barracks Ypres | 28/09/1918 | 29/09/1918 |
| War Diary | Hooge | 30/09/1918 | 30/09/1918 |
| Operation(al) Order(s) | 497th (Kent) Field Co. R.E. Operation Order No. 2 | | |
| Operation(al) Order(s) | Operation Order No 3 by 497th (Kent) Field Coy. R.E. | 13/10/1918 | 13/10/1918 |
| Miscellaneous | Transport | | |
| Miscellaneous | 497th (Kent) Field Co. R.E. Addendum To Operation Order No. 2 | | |
| Diagram etc | Legend | | |
| Heading | Herewith War Diary for October 1918, and Appendix 'A' | 05/11/1918 | 05/11/1918 |
| Miscellaneous | Appendix B | 26/09/1918 | 26/09/1918 |
| War Diary | Glencorse Wood J.14.a.3.6 | 01/10/1918 | 09/10/1918 |
| War Diary | 28/K.8.a.2.2 | 10/10/1918 | 12/10/1918 |
| War Diary | Oosthoek | 13/10/1918 | 13/10/1918 |
| War Diary | Ledeghem | 14/10/1918 | 14/10/1918 |
| War Diary | Salines | 15/10/1918 | 19/10/1918 |
| War Diary | Cuerne | 20/10/1918 | 20/10/1918 |
| War Diary | Staceghem | 21/10/1918 | 25/10/1918 |
| War Diary | Risquons-Tout | 26/10/1918 | 26/10/1918 |
| War Diary | Croix | 27/10/1918 | 31/10/1918 |
| Heading | War Diary of 497 (Kent) Field Coy RE From 1/11/18 To 30/11/18 Volume No XXXVIII | | |
| War Diary | Croix | 01/11/1918 | 06/11/1918 |
| War Diary | 29/T12a9.7 | 07/11/1918 | 07/11/1918 |
| War Diary | 29/U3a.4.7 | 08/11/1918 | 10/11/1918 |
| War Diary | Celles | 11/11/1918 | 14/11/1918 |
| War Diary | Flobecq | 15/11/1918 | 15/11/1918 |
| War Diary | Lessines | 16/11/1918 | 18/11/1918 |
| War Diary | Marcq | 19/11/1918 | 21/11/1918 |
| War Diary | Clabecq | 22/11/1918 | 23/11/1918 |
| War Diary | Couture St Germany | 24/11/1918 | 25/11/1918 |
| War Diary | Mousty | 26/11/1918 | 27/11/1918 |
| War Diary | Lerinnes | 28/11/1918 | 28/11/1918 |
| War Diary | Harlue | 29/11/1918 | 29/11/1918 |
| War Diary | La Hesbaye | 30/11/1918 | 30/11/1918 |
| Heading | 497th (Kent) Fd Coy RE Dec 1918 Vol 34 | | |
| War Diary | 1.F 32.6.3 | 01/12/1918 | 01/12/1918 |
| War Diary | Sougne | 02/12/1918 | 04/12/1918 |
| War Diary | Les Combles | 05/12/1918 | 05/12/1918 |
| War Diary | Burnenville | 06/12/1918 | 06/12/1918 |
| War Diary | Lager Elsenborn | 07/12/1918 | 07/12/1918 |
| War Diary | Imgeneroich | 08/12/1918 | 08/12/1918 |
| War Diary | Vlatten | 09/12/1918 | 09/12/1918 |
| War Diary | Erp | 10/12/1918 | 11/12/1918 |
| War Diary | Bachem | 11/12/1918 | 13/12/1918 |
| War Diary | Mulheim | 14/12/1918 | 15/12/1918 |
| War Diary | Grunau | 16/12/1918 | 19/12/1918 |
| War Diary | Burscheid | 20/12/1918 | 31/12/1918 |
| Heading | Rhine Army Southern Division Late 29th Division 497th (Kent) Fld Coy R.E. Jan-Oct 1919 | | |
| Heading | War Diary of 497th Field Coy RE From 1/1/19 To 31/1/19 Volume No 40 | | |
| War Diary | Burschied | 12/01/1919 | 24/01/1919 |
| War Diary | Burschied Cologne Bridgehead | 01/01/1919 | 11/01/1919 |
| War Diary | Burschied | 25/01/1919 | 31/01/1919 |

| | | | |
|---|---|---|---|
| Heading | War Diary of 497 Field Coy RE From 1/2/19 To 28/2/19 Volume No 41 | | |
| War Diary | Burscheid Germany | 01/02/1919 | 28/02/1919 |
| Heading | War Diary of 497th Field Coy RE From 1/5/19 To 31/5/19 Volume No 44 | | |
| War Diary | Burscheid Germany | 01/05/1919 | 31/05/1919 |
| Heading | War Diary of 497 (Kent) Field Coy RE From June 1st To June 30th Volume No 45 | | |
| War Diary | Burscheid Germany | 01/06/1919 | 30/06/1919 |
| Heading | Herewith Diary for month ending 31st July 1919 | 31/07/1919 | 31/07/1919 |
| War Diary | Burscheid Germany | 01/07/1919 | 31/07/1919 |
| Heading | Original War Diary of 497th Field Coy RE For Month Of August 1919 Volume 47 | | |
| War Diary | Burscheid Germany | 01/08/1919 | 25/08/1919 |
| War Diary | Pattscheid Germany | 26/08/1919 | 31/08/1919 |
| Heading | War Diary of 497th Field Co RE Southern Division From Sept 1st To Sept 30th/19 | | |
| War Diary | Pattscheid Germany | 01/09/1919 | 22/09/1919 |
| War Diary | Burscheid Germany | 23/09/1919 | 30/09/1919 |
| Heading | War Diary From O.C. 497 Field Company R.E. Volume No 42 From 1/10/19 To 27/10/19 | | |
| War Diary | Burscheid Germany | 01/10/1919 | 27/10/1919 |

WO/95/2293

1/2 497 (1/3 Kent) Field Conseurg
Royal Engineers

## 29TH DIVISION
## CIVIL ENGINEERS

1-3RD (KENT) FLD COY R.E
MAR 1916 - ~~~~

497TH (KENT) FLD COY R.E.
~~~~ - ~~~~

Mar 1916 — Oct 1919

FROM DARDANELLES
52 DIV TROOPS

29th Divisional Engineers

----

Arrived MARSEILLES from EGYPT 22.3.16.

1/3rd KENT

FIELD COMPANY R. E.

MARCH 1916

29

1/3 Kent Fd Coy R.E.

Vol I B.E.F
from M.E.F

# WAR DIARY
## or
## INTELLIGENCE SUMMARY.
*(Erase heading not required.)*

Army Form C. 2118.

| Place | Date | Hour | Summary of Events and Information | Remarks and references to Appendices |
|---|---|---|---|---|
| | 1916 | | | |
| | 1/3 | | Drill & knapshot signalling. | appR |
| | | | One man sick to Hospital. One man typho from KANTARA | |
| SUEZ | 2/3 | | Drill & knapshot signalling. | appR |
| do | 3/3 | | 2 men Htrn to duty from Hospital. | appR |
| | | | Drill semaphore signalling | |
| do | 4/3 | | 1 man returns to duty from Hospital | appR |
| | | | Drill knapshot signalling. Present strength of Co. 5 officers 195 other ranks | appR |
| do | 5/3 | 0700 | 45 men Mounted Section leave SUEZ | |
| | | | 1 man sick to Hospital | appR |
| | | | Church Parade. | appR |
| do | 6/3 | | 3 men return to duty from Hospital. | appR |
| do | 7/3 | | 2 men return to duty from Hospital | appR |
| do | 8/3 | | 2 men return to duty from Hospital | appR |
| do | 9/3 | | 38 men of Co. disinfected | appR |
| | | | 1 man leaves on charge of Horse | |
| do | 10/3 | | Remainder of Co. disinfected | appR |
| do | 11/3 | | 6 or 7 men sent to Hospital. One man to duty from Hospital. Present strength of Co. 5 o. + 55 o.r. | appR |

# WAR DIARY
## or
## INTELLIGENCE SUMMARY.
(Erase heading not required.)

Army Form C. 2118.

Instructions regarding War Diaries and Intelligence Summaries are contained in F.S. Regs., Part II. and the Staff Manual respectively. Title pages will be prepared in manuscript.

| Place | Date | Hour | Summary of Events and Information | Remarks and references to Appendices |
|---|---|---|---|---|
| | 1916 | | | |
| SUEZ CAMP | 12/3 | | 1 man sick to hospital. | OC/R |
| | 13/3 | | Orders received that Co. is to embark on HMT SLAVONIA @ SUEZ @ 1130 on following day. | OC/R |
| | 14/3 | | 1 man returns to duty from hospital | |
| | | 1130 | Co. embarks on HMT SLAVONIA. Strength 5 officers, 155 other ranks +5 attached. | OC/R |
| HMT SLAVONIA | 15/3 | 1500 | HMT SLAVONIA sails. | OC/R |
| | 16/3 | 0830 | arrive PORT SAID | OC/R |
| | 17/3 | 0800 | sails from Port Said | 20C/R |
| | 18/3 | | Strength of Co.: 5 officers, 155 O. ranks Cpt. +5 LONDON R.E. attd. | OC/R |
| | 19/3 | | | OC/R |
| | 20/3 | | | OC/R |
| | 21/3 | | | OC/R |
| | 22/3 | | S.S. SLAVONIA arrives MARSEILLES + to berthed about 1800 | |
| MARSEILLES | | 1624 | Lt MORGAN and 23 O.R. leave by train in charge of COMPANY baggage | |
| | | 2112 | Remainder of Co. leave by train (including 5 1/2 LONDON FD CO R.E.) | OC/R |
| | | | 1 man sick to HOSPITAL | OC/R |

# WAR DIARY
## — or —
## INTELLIGENCE SUMMARY.
(Erase heading not required.)

Army Form C. 2118.

| Place | Date | Hour | Summary of Events and Information | Remarks and references to Appendices |
|---|---|---|---|---|
| | 1916 | | | |
| IN TRAIN | 23/3 | | — | Coy/R |
| | 24/3 | | — | Coy/R |
| MONFIERES | 25/3 | 0030 | COMPANY arrived PONT REMY (1 man sent to hospital sick) and proceeded to billets at MONFIERES, which were reported by L.M. ARGEN + 23 other ranks. Details of A.H. of MOUNTED SECTION who proceeded on advance on 5/3 (45 mm) + 9/3 (Major) 2 men taken sick to hospital on 13/3 + 15/3: 3) Medic 29 draughts + 2 fatigue Men sent in Kamel 5 men at LONDON FD.CO RE when + field unit. [Remy had having been moved off SUEZ - Loan + Reserve] | Coy/R |
| | | | 3 men sent to 611/E Supplies Army (88th Bde) | Coy/R |
| do | 26/3 | | 3 men sick to hospital. Present strength of Co. 5 Officers 194 O.R. + 1 in hospital. | Coy/R |
| do | 27/3 | | 2 men sick to hospital | Coy/R |
| do | 28/3 | | 3 men sick to hospital | |
| | | | 1 man sent to ROUEN for work with in RE RECORDS (29th DIVN) 3rd ECHELON | |
| | | | 1 Pvt horse returned from 1/2nd LONDON FD. CO. R.E. | |
| do | 29/3 | | 1 man sent to BELLE ÉGLISE to act as draughtsman in office of C.E. VIII Corps. | Coy/R |
| | | | 1 A.S.C. driver sent to Co. to take percentage of the R.E. in flying movement of Co. | |

# WAR DIARY
## INTELLIGENCE SUMMARY.
*(Erase heading not required.)*

Army Form C. 2118.

| Place | Date | Hour | Summary of Events and Information | Remarks and references to Appendices |
|---|---|---|---|---|
| MONFLIÈRES | 1/6 | | 1 Driver ASC temporarily attached to Coy. | |
| | 29/3 | | 2 Army draught horses temporarily attached to Coy. | |
| | | | 1 man returns to duty from Hospital. | O34/R |
| do | 30/3 | 0900 | Coy. moves out of billets @ MONFLIÈRES into billets at SURCAMP - marching via AILLY + BRUCAMP | |
| SURCAMP | | | 1 Driver return to duty from Hospital | |
| | | | 2 additional draught horses drawn from No.2 ADVANCED REMOUNT DEPOT | |
| | | | 3 men attached to 86th BDE train now attached to 86th BDE. TRAIN. | |
| do | 31/3 | 0615 | Coy. moves out of billets @ SURCAMP into billets @ BEAUVAL - marching via DOMMERT, BERNEUIL, FIENVILLERS + CANDAS | O34/R |
| BEAUVAL | | 1215 | Arrived BEAUVAL | O34/R |
| | | | 1 man returns from attachment to 86th BDE TRAIN | |

O.G. Ruston Major R.E. (T)
O.C. 1/3rd KENT FD. CO. RE

29th Divisional Engineers

------

1/3rd KENT

FIELD COMPANY R. E.

APRIL 1 9 1 6

29

1/3 Kent Fd Coy
R.E.
Vol II

# WAR DIARY

## INTELLIGENCE SUMMARY.

Army Form C. 2118.

| Place | Date | Hour | Summary of Events and Information | Remarks and references to Appendices |
|---|---|---|---|---|
| | 1916 | | | |
| BEAUVAL | 1/4 | | 1 man sick to Hospital. | A/R |
| do | 2/4 | | 1 man sick to Hospital. Present strength of Bn.: 5 officers, 1 interpreter, 187 o.r. [+ 1 ASC attached] {69 rest animals incl. 2 attd by 86th Bde.} | A/R |
| do | 3/4 | | Test evacuation of billets by 86th Bde. 1 man sick to Hospital & returned to duty. | A/R |
| do | 4/4 | | 1/Lt KITCHING to No. 4 CASUALTY CLEARING STATION (This received from 86th Bde. last move on fully day (copy attached) 1 man sick to Hospital. | APPENDIX I |
| | | 0935 | C.O. moves to ENGLEBELMER via BEAUQUESNE, ACHEUX, FORCEVILLE & HEDAUVILLE 60 km. ACHEUX with Bde. At MARIEUX, Bde. was mobilled by CORPS. CMDR. as it marched past | |
| | | 1945 | Arrived destination. Transport left @ ACHEUX with 1 officer in charge. 1 man returns to duty from Hospital. 1 man returned to duty from Hospital. | A/R |
| do | 5/4 | | G.S. Wagon returned to A.S.C., 1 man & heavy draft horses cease to be attached to Bn. Distribn of Bn: 4/4 : ACHEUX 48 ENGELBELMER 130 5/4 : ACHEUX 49 ENGELBELMER 143 | A/R |

# WAR DIARY
## INTELLIGENCE SUMMARY
(Erase heading not required.)

Army Form C. 2118.

Instructions regarding War Diaries and Intelligence Summaries are contained in F. S. Regs., Part II. and the Staff Manual respectively. Title pages will be prepared in manuscript.

| Place | Date | Hour | Summary of Events and Information | Remarks and references to Appendices |
|---|---|---|---|---|
| ENGELBEL-MER | 1916 6/4 | morn. | Went round FORTS. CRE received instructions as to work to be carried on by Co. there & elsewhere. | copy R |
| | | aft. | Allocated work on FORTS to No.3 Section & took Section Cmdr. round with Co. 200 Infantry on works. 2 men return to duty from hospital. Distrib.n of Co.: ACHEUX: 48. ENGELBELMER: 146 | copy R |
| do | 7/4 | Noon | Instructions received from C.R.E. to press on work in REDOUBT LINE. No.4 Section detached It. to work on REDOUBT LINE with No.3 Section. 370 Infantry on works. 3 men return to duty from hospital. | |
| | | | 1 man attached to R.E.'s D.Staff as draughtsman (Lieut. 3off.) Dist.n of Co.: ACHEUX: 10 + 48 I.F. ENGLEBELMER: 143 + 6 I.F. | copy R |
| do | 8/4 | | 400 infantry on works. 1 man attached to CREs Staff as clerk, WARRAM 1 man returns to duty from Hospital. 1 Officer (Lieut. BUCKLEY) temporarily attached to Co. | copy R |

# WAR DIARY or INTELLIGENCE SUMMARY.

Army Form C. 2118.

| Place | Date | Hour | Summary of Events and Information | Remarks and references to Appendices |
|---|---|---|---|---|
| ENGLE- BELMER | 10/6 8/4 | | 1 Officer (Lt. MORGAN) Transferred from ACHEUX to ENGLEBELMER. Distribution of Co.: Hq.; 50; 1 Sect. + 144 O.R.; ACHEUX: 47 | OS/R |
| do | 9/4 | 9am | Aerial lecture redemonstration of use of Antigas Helmets, Co. attended. 40 infantry on works Conference of Co. Cmdrs. at C.R.E. | |
| | | 15:00 | 2 men sick to Hospital Present strength of Co. 5 O., 1 Infantry, 169 O.R. Distribution: HQ.: 5 O., 1 Sect. + 142 O.R.; ACHEUX: 47 O.R. | OS/R |
| do | 10/4 | | Distribution as per day | OS/R |
| do | 11/4 | | do | OS/R |
| do | 12/4 | | do | |
| do | 13/4 | | 14 A.C.C. attached for works. Distribution: 5 Officers, 1 Sect. + 159 O.R.; Hq.; ACHEUX: 44 O.R. | OS/R |
| do | 14/4 | | Distribution as previous day REDOUBT LINE works handed over to G.O.C. Rt. Bde. | OS/R OS/R |
| do | 15/4 | | Distribution: HQ. 5 Officers, 1 Sect., 161 O.R (incl. 14 ACC att.); ACHEUX: 42. | OS/R OS/R |

# WAR DIARY
## INTELLIGENCE SUMMARY

Army Form C. 2118.

| Place | Date | Hour | Summary of Events and Information | Remarks and references to Appendices |
|---|---|---|---|---|
| ENGLE-BEL-MER | 1916 16/4 | | Work commenced on dug outs for Inft and Reserve lines (see Appendix) Distribution of Co. as previous day. Strength: 5 officers, 1 interpreter, + 263 other ranks. Animals: 4 riding, 32 draught, 4 pack mules, 27 ordinary mules. | APPENDIX N°1 |
| do | 17/4 | | Lt. D.R. WILLIAMSON R.E. attached to Co. + posted to N°2 Section. M.O. 1 man (R.E. staff) attached to Co. for rations. Distribution: H.Q.; 6 offrs, 1 Inter. +147 O.R. (1 Cyclist +2 R.E. attached for rations) ACHEUX: 42. | OC 4/R OC 4/R |
| do | 18/4 | | 1 man returns to duty from hospital. | OC 4/R |
| do | 19/4 | | 1 officer + 60 O.R. (Mining party) attached to Co. for work stations. Distribution: H.Q.: 7 offrs, 1 Interpreter, + 224 O.R. ACHEUX: 42 O.R. | OC 4/R |
| do | 13/4 | 1800 | 1 Lt BUCKLEY + N°4 Section attached to 88th Bde. for work in Frankfort lines. Distribution: H.Q. 7 offrs, 1 Inter, 227 O.R. (incl. O.R.S.) ACHEUX: 39 O.R. | OC 4/R |
| do | 19/4 | | " 60 previous day | OC 4/R |
| do | 20/4 | | Distribution H.Q. 7 offrs, 1 Inter, 227 O.R. (incl. O.R.S.) ACHEUX: 32 O.R. | OC 4/R |
| do | 21/4 | | Lt MORGAN sick to hospital. Distribution H.Q. 6 offrs, 1 Inter, 225 O.R. ACHEUX: 38 O.R. | OC 4/R |

# WAR DIARY
## INTELLIGENCE SUMMARY.
*(Erase heading not required.)*

Army Form C. 2118.

| Place | Date | Hour | Summary of Events and Information | Remarks and references to Appendices |
|---|---|---|---|---|
| ENGLEBELMER | 1916 | | | |
| | 22/4 | | Distribution of the various duty. | 004/R |
| | 23/4 | | Do. Previous day. (In fusilic for an hour) | 005/R |
| | 24/4 | | " H.Q. party menaced by I man (C.R.E. staff) attached for return | 006/R |
| | 25/4 | | L.t MORGAN returns to duty from Hospital. | |
| | | | Date: H.Q. 6 Offrs N.C.M. 0 230 O.R. ACHEUX: 36 O.R. | |
| | | | 1 man attached R.F.A. for return. | |
| | | | 2 Grenadiers attached R.G. for instruction man of Bangalore Torpedo. | |
| | | | Went round works with C.R.E. | 007/R |
| | 26/4 | | Lt MORGAN to Hospital Sick | |
| | | | Men [crossed out] [trained] for mining: 26 O.Ranks | |
| | | | [Men] for instruction in manufacture of Bangalore Torpedo: 3 O.R. | |
| | | | Date: H.Q. 6 Offrs 0 260 O.R. ACHEUX: 37 O.R. | |
| | | | Notes adopted in manufacture of Bangalore Torpedo (see Appendix) | Appendix No 2 / 008/R |
| | 27/4 | | 2 men wounded (slightly) to Hospital from H.Q. | |
| | 28/4 | | 3 men attached for no to Tom to Torpedo return to this Unit. | |
| | | | 1 man sick to Hospital of ACHEUX | |

Army Form C. 2118.

# WAR DIARY
## INTELLIGENCE SUMMARY.
*(Erase heading not required.)*

Instructions regarding War Diaries and Intelligence Summaries are contained in F. S. Regs., Part II. and the Staff Manual respectively. Title pages will be prepared in manuscript.

| Place | Date | Hour | Summary of Events and Information | Remarks and references to Appendices |
|---|---|---|---|---|
| | 4/16 | | | |
| ENGLEBELMER | 28 | | Distribution: H.Q. 6 Offrs, 255 O.R. ACHEUX: 36 O.R. | O.C.R |
| | 29 | | 1 Man sick to Hospital. | O.C.R |
| | 30 | | Det. H.Q. 6 Officers, 260 O.R. ACHEUX: 30 O.R. 2 O.R. attached for instruction rejoin unit fr. H.Q. Present Strength of Co.: Company: 5 Officers, 167 O.R. Attached "Cyclists": 14 O.R. Music: 1 Officer, 86 O.R. B.4 Staff: 3 O.R. | |
| | | 1500 | C.R.E. Conference | O.C.R |

O.C.R Ruston
Major R.E.(T)
O.C. 1/3rd Kent Fwd. Co. R.E.
1/5/16

DEEP DUG OUTS          APPENDIX N° 1
                            APRIL 1916

Two types are being made (a) for standing only
(b) for sleeping.

(a) These allow 4 superficial feet per man & are
placed only in support line under the parados
as shown in sketch below.

                                            Not to scale

Section of one dug out

                    Round Timber

                    6' 3"

                                        Not to scale.

Mem:
Galleries are run down behind traverses & joined up by
dugouts 3' of passage way being placed to right or left of
gallery before dug out proper is commenced. The dug outs
are made as large as the distance between traverses
allows. Galleries are made 5'6" high by 2' wide in the clear.

APPENDIX Nº 1
APRIL 1916

(b) Sleeping dug outs are made in a similar way to standing dug outs; this type of dug out is placed in Reserve line. They are made as long as distance apart of traverses allows (see Mem. at foot of (a)) but are 8' wide with a sleeping bench of rabbit netting.

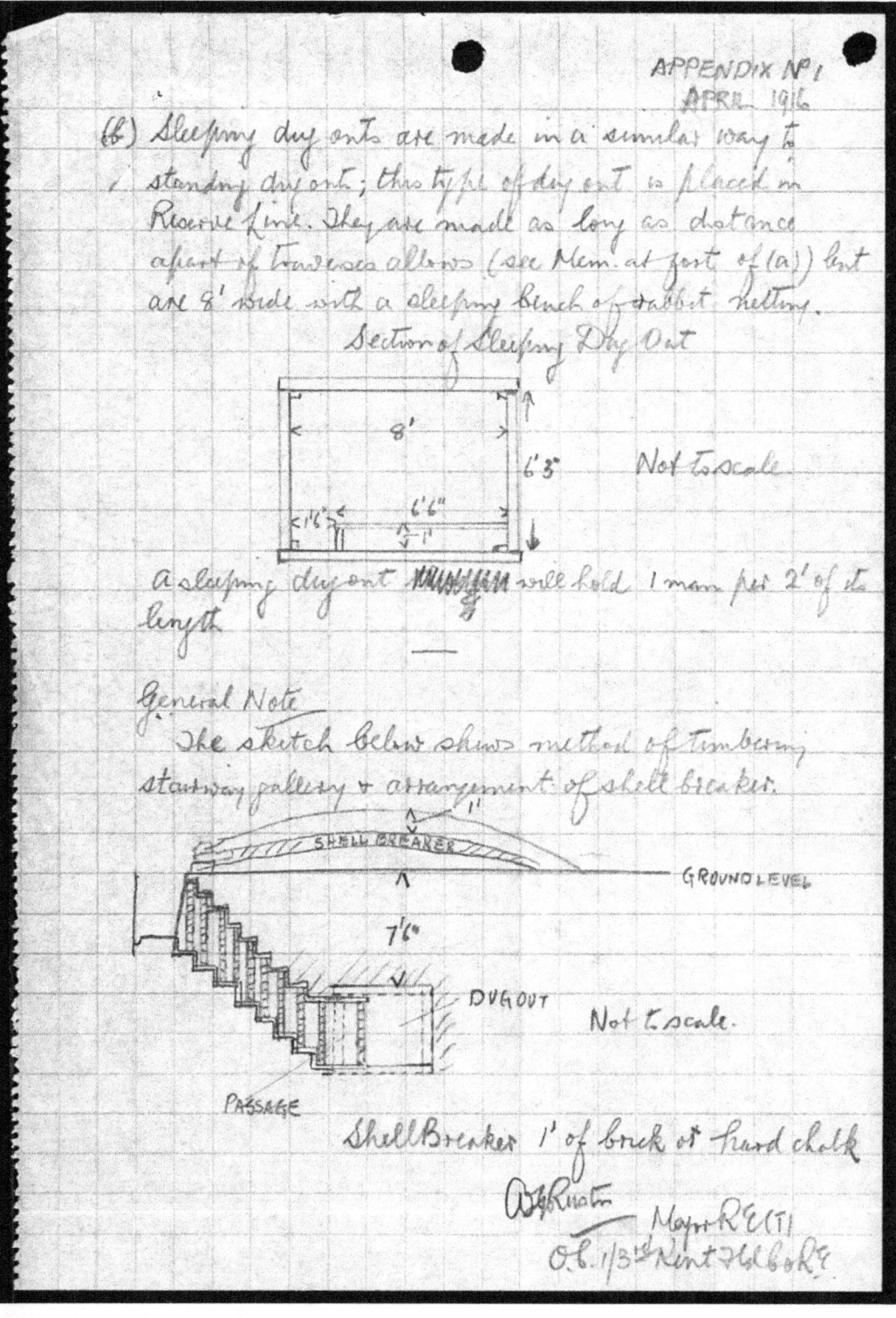

Section of Sleeping Dug Out

Not to scale.

A sleeping dug out will hold 1 man per 2' of its length.

General Note

The sketch below shows method of timbering stairway gallery & arrangement of shell breaker.

Not to scale.

Shell Breaker 1' of brick or hard chalk

A.E. Ruston
Major R.E.(T)
O.C. 1/3rd Kent Fd Co. R.E.

APPENDIX Nº 2
APL. 1916 141 (i)

## BANGALORE TORPEDO.

The Torpedo was made of a number of lengths of 2½" Zinc Pipe fitted together & loaded with Ammonal. The pipes were of standard length of 6' & were so made that any number desired could be used according to the width of the entanglement which it was desired to cut.

Each length of pipe was slightly constricted at the front end & slightly widened at the rear end so as to enable the front end of one pipe to be pushed 6 inches into the rear of another pipe. (See sketch.)

```
<-5"-> TAPERED               <-C"-> ENLARGED
[====Ammonal===]=          [////////////] -WOOD PLUG
ZINC DIAPHRAGM                     NAIL 6" from FACE of PLUG.
      <----6'---->
```

A zinc diaphragm was soldered on to the front end of each. When the pipe had been carefully filled with Ammonal well rammed to within 6" or so of top of pipe a wooden plug was inserted to enable pipe to be carried in any position without spilling explosive. The two nails were intended to act as a gauge shewing how near to top of Ammonal had been filled, i.e. insure that a little less than 6" of pipe was unfilled.

The Nose of the Torpedo was fitted with a wooden Nose Cap of such a shape as enable Torpedo to be pushed under or through barbed wire without difficulty (see sketch p. ii)

APPENDIX No 2
APL 1916 /141 (ii)

NOSE CAP [sketch of nose cap]

The Nose cap was made to fit snugly on to the front end of any of the pipes.

The device for detonating the torpedo was a plug of wood fitted at the fore end with a 1 oz G.C. Primer half let into the plug, with a detonator in the primer & a length of safety fuze (abt 10") leading through centre of plug to a Nobel's fuze lighter (see sketch)

WOOD PLUG — SAFETY FUZE
— FUZE LIGHTER
PRIMER with DETONATOR
AMMONAL

It was found that when wooden plugs were removed from rear end of pipe the ammonal remained undisturbed unless the pipe were tapped or jerked somewhat forcibly, so that it was decided to dispense with a second disc closing the pipe 6" from its rear end, the presence of which caused sufficient discontinuity in charge to prevent a successful explosion of a series of lengths of pipe.

It was arranged that each torpedo party should have a spare detonating plug to allow for a miss fire.

A.S.H. Ruston
Major R.E. (T)
OC 1/3 Kent Fd Co R.E.

29

Appendix to Vol I
1/3 Kent Fd Coy
R.E.

OR 31.

From:- O.C. /3rd Kent Field Coy R.E.

To:- Officer i/c. A.G's. Office.
    Base B.E.F.

The attached was omitted when sending War Diary for month of March.

A.H. Ruston

Major R.E.(T)
OC/3º Kent Field Co. R.E.

11/4/16.

S E C R E T.

1/3ᵈ KENT FD. CO. R.E. WAR DIARY
APPENDIX 1 Apl. 1916      Copy No 9

86TH BRIGADE OPERATION ORDER NO.44
---------------------------------

BEAUVAL.
2-4-16.

Ref.Map 1/80,000 Set B Sheet 12.

1. The Brigade will move into the Divisional Reserve Area on the 4th inst. in accordance with attached March Table "A".

2. Order of march as under:-

   Brigade Headquarters.        Pass S.P at 0930
   Machine Gun Company.
   Royal Munster Fusiliers.
   Royal Dublin Fusiliers.
   Lancashire Fusiliers.
   Royal Fusiliers.
   Kent Field Company, R.E.
   89th Field Ambulance.        Pass S.P at 1000
   Train waggons.

?955
 920

3. Head of column to pass junction of BEAUVAL-DOULLENS Road and the Northerly BEAUVAL-BEAUQUESNE Road at 0930.

4. There will be an hour and 10 minutes halt for dinners; time notified en route.

5. One Officer per Battalion will be detailed to collect the stragglers of his Unit and bring them on in a formed body.

   In addition one platoon of 2nd Royal Fusiliers will be detailed as rearguard to assist in this duty.

6. On reaching the vicinity of ACHEUX Units must be prepared to ~~take military precautions if~~ to be subjected to shell fire.

   Formed bodies of troops must not enter BEAUSSART and ENGLEBELMER until after dusk.

7. The Refilling Point on April 5th will be on ACHEUX-LEALVILLERS Road.

8. Orders re destination of transport of BEAUSSART and ENGLEBELMER Units to be given verbally.

Issued at........1330

Ian Grant            Capt.,
Bde Major, 86th Brigade.

Copy No. 1-2 War Diary           8. Bde Machine Gun Co.
         3   Office              9. Kent Field Co.R.E.
         4   Royal Fus.         10. 89th Field Ambulance
         5   Lancashire Fus.    11. No.2 Co. A.S.C.
         6   R.Munster Fus      12. 29 Div (for information)
         7   R.Dublin Fus.

Pt. APPENDIX I
WAR DIARY of 1/3rd
KENT FD. CO. R.E. for
Apl. 1916

## MARCH TABLE "A"

| UNIT | FROM | TO | VIA | REMARKS |
|---|---|---|---|---|
| 86th Brigade Headquarters<br>Brigade Machine GUN CO.<br>R.Dublin Fusrs.<br>Lancashire Fusrs.<br>89th Field Ambulance | BEAUVAL | ACHEUX | BEAUQUESNE<br>MARIEUX<br>LOUVENCOURT | |
| R.Munster Fusrs. | " | BEAUSSART | BEAUQUESNE<br>MARIEUX<br>LOUVENCOURT<br>ACHEUX<br>FORCEVILLE | Halting under cover until dusk on clearing ACHEUX if situation demands. |
| Royal Fusrs.<br>Kent Field Co. R.E. | " | ENGLEBELMER | BEAUQUESNE<br>MARIEUX<br>LOUVENCOURT<br>ACHEUX<br>FORCEVILLE<br>MESDAUVILLE | Halting under cover until dusk on clearing ACHEUX if situation demands. |

29th Divisional Enginners

-------

1/3rd KENT

FIELD COMPANY R. E.

MAY 1916

1/3 Kent 2⁰ Copy R.E.

Army Form C. 2118.

# WAR DIARY
## INTELLIGENCE SUMMARY
(Erase heading not required.)

Vol 3

| Place | Date | Hour | Summary of Events and Information | Remarks and references to Appendices |
|---|---|---|---|---|
| ENGLEBEL-MER | 1916 | | | |
| | 1/5 | | Distribution of Coy: H.Q.: 259 & Toffre. ACHEUX: 29 O.R. | OC/R |
| | 2/5 | | 1 man returned to duty from Hospital (ACHEUX section) | OC/R |
| | 3/5 | | Dist. of Coy: H.Q. 60ffo + 260 O.R. ACHEUX 29 O.R. | |
| | | | Dist. as previous day | OC/R |
| | 4/5 | | Bde. change: 87ᵗʰ ᵃ/ᵗᵃᶜʰᵉᵈ 85ᵗʰ Bde in R. sector of Divisional front. | OC/R |
| | | | 10 R. (KENT FLD. CO.) 1 O.R. (b/ACC.) to Hospital sick | OC/R |
| | | | Distn: H.Q. Section of Coy. Midnight By ⚡ | OC/R |
| | ⚡ | | 1 O.R. ACC. attached Coy sman sick to Hospital | |
| | 5/5 | | 1 Officer returns from leave. | |
| | | | Distn: H.Q. increased by 1 Laputa. | |
| | 6/5 | | 1 Officer + 1 O.R. attached to Bde. (Officers' Instructor) | |
| | 7/5 | | 1 Man returns to duty from Hospital | |
| | | | Streng. of Coy: Officers 5/5 + 2 attached 12 Laputa. | |
| | | | O.R.: 16ffo + 105 attached (89 Noms, 14 Bychoo, 3 & R.E. Dump Staff, 2 Ba----) 262 O.R. ACHEUX: 29 O.R. | |
| | 8/5 | | Distn: H.Q.: 70ffo, 1 Laputa + 262 O.R. ACHEUX: 29 O.R. | OC/R |
| | | | 1 O.R. (from H.Q.) sick to Hospital. | |

Army Form C. 2118.

# WAR DIARY
## INTELLIGENCE SUMMARY
(Erase heading not required.)

Instructions regarding War Diaries and Intelligence Summaries are contained in F.S. Regs., Part II. and the Staff Manual respectively. Title pages will be prepared in manuscript.

| Place | Date | Hour | Summary of Events and Information | Remarks and references to Appendices |
|---|---|---|---|---|
| ENGLEBEL MER | 8/5 | | 1/2 Kent W.J. TURNER and P. NEILL join Company | OO/R |
| | 9/5 | | 1 NCO & 8 men attached to 86th Bde. | |
| | | | 1 O.R. discharged from Hospital to duty (ACHEUX) | OO/R |
| | | | Distn: HQ: 9 Offrs, 1 Lt Spprs, 252 O.R. ACHEUX: 30 O.R. | OO/R |
| | 10/5 | | Distn as previous day | |
| | 11/5 | | 1/Lt. J.L.C. HALL goes on leave. | OO/R |
| | | | 'A' Coy of 2nd MONMOUTHSHIRE REGT. provided for pioneer training north of 1/3 KENT F.O. CO. R.E. | OO/R |
| | | | Distn: HQ: 8 Offrs, 1 Lt Sppr, 263 O.R. ACHEUX: 29 O.R. | OO/R |
| | 12/5 | | 1 O.R. from H.Q. to Hospital | |
| | | | 1 O.R. from Mining Detachment to Hospital | OO/R |
| | 13/5 | | Distn HQ: 8 Offrs, 1 Sppr, 254 O.R. ACHEUX: 24 O.R. | |
| | | | 1 O.R. returns to duty from Hospital | |
| | 14/5 | | Distn. HQ. 8 Offrs, 1 Sppr, 261 O.R. ACHEUX: 20 O.R. | OO/R |
| | 15/5 | | Distn. as previous day | OO/R |
| | 16/5 | | 1 man sick to Hospital from ACHEUX. Lt WILLIAMSON R.E. rejoins his unit (1/2 LONDON FD. CO. R.E.) | OO/R |
| | 17/5 | | 1 Offr & 121 O.R. (A.C.C.) attached to Coy for work. | |

# WAR DIARY or INTELLIGENCE SUMMARY.

Army Form C. 2118.

| Place | Date | Hour | Summary of Events and Information | Remarks and references to Appendices |
|---|---|---|---|---|
| ENGLEBEL-MER | 16/5 | | | |
| | 17/5 | | 1 O.R. returns to duty from Hospital (ACHEUX) | O&R |
| | 18/5 | | Distrib. Two 8 O/c/rs, 12 Interpr. + 282 O.R. @ H.Q.; 20 @ ACHEUX | O&R |
| | 19/5 | | Distribution 8 Offrs., 19 Interprs. + 283 O.R. @ H.Q.; 20 @ ACHEUX | O&R |
| | | | ACHEUX detachment joins H.Q. at ENGLEBELMER. | |
| | | | 1 O.R. to Hospital. | O&R |
| | 20/5 | | 9 O.R. attached to Bde in Front line relieved by same number | O&R |
| | | | 1 attached O.R. (Miner) Hospital | O&R |
| | 21/5 | | 1 Officer (attached for instruction) + 1 O.R. (servant) return to their unit | O&R |
| | 22/5 | | 1 O.R. sick to Hospital | O&R |
| | | | 1 O.R. " " " | O&R |
| | | | 2/Lt D.W. MORGAN, 1/2nd Monmouthshire Regt., reported to Co. for instruction, 1 O.R. (servant) also attached to Co. | |
| | 23/5 | | — | O&R |
| | 24/5 | | Lt SIMPSON of 1/1st WEST RIDING FIELD CO. R.E. joins for duty. | |
| | | | 2 O.R. return to duty from Hospital | O&R |

**WAR DIARY**
or
**INTELLIGENCE SUMMARY.**
(Erase heading not required.)

Army Form C. 2118.

| Place | Date | Hour | Summary of Events and Information | Remarks and references to Appendices |
|---|---|---|---|---|
| Englebelmer | 1916 | | | |
| | 25/5 | | I.O.R. returns to duty from Hospital | J.H.S. |
| | 26/5 | | Lieut P.R.J. Morgan returns to duty from Hospital & 2.O.R. | J.H.S. |
| | 27/5 | | I.O.R. admitted to Hospital | J.H.S. |
| | 28/5 | | — | |
| | 29/5 | | 2nd Lieut C.J. Betts S.W.B. & 9.O.R. attached for work & rations | J.H.S. |
| | | | I.O.R. (mining party) returns to duty from Hospital | |
| | 30/5 | | I.O.R. returns to duty from Hospital | |
| | | | I.O.R. (mining party) returns to duty from Hospital | |
| | | | 37119 Lance Corpl Morgan, H.P. sent for instruction in Gas. | J.H.S. |
| | 31/5 | | I.O.R. (mining party) returns to duty from Hospital | J.H.S. |
| | | | I.O.R. (mining party) admitted to hospital for dental treatment | J.H.S. |

J.H. Simpson
Lieut R.E.(T)
for O.C. 1st Kent Field Coy R.E.

29th Divisional Engineers

1/3rd KENT

FIELD COMPANY R. E.

JUNE 1916

1/3 Kent Fd Coy RE

# WAR DIARY
## or
## INTELLIGENCE SUMMARY.

Army Form C. 2118.

Vol 4

| Place | Date | Hour | Summary of Events and Information | Remarks and references to Appendices |
|---|---|---|---|---|
| | 1916 | | | |
| ENGLEBEL-MER | 1/6 | | London Gazette 1 June — 2nd Lt (Temp Lt) P.R.J. MORGAN to be Temp. Capt. (29 Oct 1915) vice L.C. HALL to be [Temp Lt (29 Oct 1915)] | copy R |
| | 2/6 | | 371 & 2 G.R. MORGAN, H.P. returns from Base house | copy R |
| | 3/6 | | — | copy R |
| | 4/6 | | 1 O.R. (S.W.B.) to Hospital | |
| | | | On 25/5/16 2/Lt CARDEW (A.C.C.) ceased to be attached to Co., he is now about that date the 33 R.E. attached to Co. & 6 were transferred from A.C.C. to 2nd S.W.B. | |
| | | | Strength of Co: 5 officers 182 O.R. attached: 2 officers (M.R. R.E.), 10 + 60 O.R. (MINERS), 10 + 41 O.R. (2nd S.W.B.), 10 + 10 O.R. (MONMOUTHS) | copy R |
| | 5/6 | | 1 O.R. (MINERS) to Hospital | |
| | | | 1 O.R. attached to 1/2 LONDON FLD CO. for FIELD PUNISHMENT. | |
| | | | 10 + 41 O.R. (MONMOUTHS) cease to be attached to Co. | |
| | | | Capt. P.R.J. MORGAN proceeds on leave. | |
| | 6/6 | | O.C. Co. returns from leave | copy R |
| | | | — | copy R |

Army Form C. 2118.

# WAR DIARY
## or
## INTELLIGENCE SUMMARY.
*(Erase heading not required.)*

Instructions regarding War Diaries and Intelligence Summaries are contained in F.S. Regs., Part II. and the Staff Manual respectively. Title pages will be prepared in manuscript.

| Place | Date | Hour | Summary of Events and Information | Remarks and references to Appendices |
|---|---|---|---|---|
| ENGLEBEL MER | 1916 7/6 | — | | O.S.4.R |
| | 8/6 | — | Lt SIMPSON rejoins his unit (1/1st W RIDING FLD. CO. R.E.) | O.S.4.R |
| | 9/6 | — | 1 N.C.O. sick to Hospital. | O.S.4.R |
| | 10/6 | — | | O.S.4.R |
| | 11/6 | — | | O.S.4.R |
| | 12/6 | — | 10.R. admitted to Hospital. | O.S.4.R |
| | | — | 10.R. (S.W.B. attached) returns from Hospital | O.S.4.R |
| | 13/6 | — | | O.S.4.R |
| | 14/6 | — | 10.R. (Mining det. attached) admitted Hospital | O.S.4.R |
| | | — | 10.R. returns to duty. | O.S.4.R |
| | 15/6 | — | | O.S.4.R |
| | 16/6 | — | Capt. P.R.J. MORGAN returns from leave | O.S.4.R |
| | 17/6 | — | 10.R. (Mining detachment attached) returned to duty from admitted Hospital | O.S.4.R |
| | 18/6 | — | 10.R. ( " ) returned O.S.4.R | O.S.4.R |
| | | — | | |
| | 19/6 | — | 10.R. admitted Hospital | O.S.4.R |

# WAR DIARY
## INTELLIGENCE SUMMARY.

Army Form C. 2118.

| Place | Date | Hour | Summary of Events and Information | Remarks and references to Appendices |
|---|---|---|---|---|
| | 1916 | | | |
| ENGLEBEL-MER | 20/6 | | — | OO7/R |
| | 21/6 | | 1 Offr + 72 O.R. (A.6.6.) attached to Co. for rations, for work in Corps O.P. VIII | OO7/R |
| | 22/6 | | — | OO7/R |
| | 23/6 | | In accordance with orders from C.R.E. following movements took place:— | |
| | | | 1st Line Transport (less A double tool cart - loaded -, 1 Battle wagon - loaded, 14 pack mules) + 47 O.R. (Mounted Section + Workshop, Saddlers + Shoeing + Batt Smith) move to ACHEUX | |
| | | | 1 Orderly sent to C.R.E.'s office @ ACHEUX | |
| | | | 3 O.R. sent to join staff of C.R.E. Dump ENGLEBELMER | |
| | | | { St HALL 10. + 22 O.R. sent with lorries to maintain Dist. Light Rail to South Section of Tramways | |
| | | | { Lt BUCKLEY 10. + 10 O.R. " " " Down + North " | OO7/R |
| | | | { Lt TURNER 10. + 12 O.R. " " " Forward Water Supply | OO7/R |
| | | | in Co. lines during bombardment | |
| | | | Work done by Co.: improvement of track roads. | |
| | 24/6 | 0600 | U day. Bombardment of enemy lines started. | |
| | | | In accordance with orders from C.R.E. 1 Offr (2Lt P. NEILL) + 2 O.R. (being 10% reserve) move to ACHEUX | OO7/R |

# WAR DIARY
## or
## INTELLIGENCE SUMMARY.
(Erase heading not required.)

Army Form C. 2118.

| Place | Date | Hour | Summary of Events and Information | Remarks and references to Appendices |
|---|---|---|---|---|
| | 1916 | | | |
| ENGLEBEL-MER | 24/6 | 1800 | Co. moved out of billets into bivouacs to WEST of ENGLEBELMER leaving 1 O.R. (Stockups) in charge of Co. Dump & 4 O.R. (2nd Cpl Dolan) in charge of tool carts. 1 O.R. slightly wounded. | copy R |
| BIVOUACS | 25/6 | | V day. Work done: improvement of bivouacs & road, rapid wiring practice. 1 O.R. sick to Hospital. | copy R |
| | 26/6 | | W day. Work done: continuous day & erection of pumping plant at Well near HEDAUVILLE - ENGLEBELMER ROAD | copy R |
| | 27/6 | | X day. Work done: rapid wiring practice, road repairs, pumping plant, O.P. in Tree to AUCHONVILLERS ROAD commenced. | copy R |
| | 28/6 | | Y day. Reinforcing draft of 17 O.R. arrive from base. 1 O.R. discharged from Hospital & Rejoined = Dvl Reserve Co. Work done: Grapednoning practice, road repairs, pumping plant, O.P. in tree finished. 2 day put off 48 hours. The intercepted days being between Y1 + Y2 | copy R |

# WAR DIARY
## INTELLIGENCE SUMMARY
*(Erase heading not required.)*

Army Form C. 2118.

| Place | Date | Hour | Summary of Events and Information | Remarks and references to Appendices |
|---|---|---|---|---|
| ENGLEBEL-MER BIVOUACS | 1916 29/6 | | Y1 day. Work done: road repairs. | ozyR |
| | 30/6 | | Y2 day. 1 O.R. sick to Hospital. 2 O.R. join Reserve Detachment @ ACHEUX. Work done: road repairs. | ozyR |

ozyRnolan
Major R.E. (?)
O.C. 1/3rd Kent Fd.Co. R.E.

25th Divisional Engineers

--------

1/3rd KENT

FIELD COMPANY R. E.

JULY 1916

CONFIDENTIAL

WAR DIARY

of

1/3RD KENT FIELD COMPANY R.E.,(T.F.)

from 1st to 31st July, 1916.

------------------

VOLUME X

------------------

# WAR DIARY
## INTELLIGENCE SUMMARY.
*(Erase heading not required.)*

Army Form C. 2118.

1/3 KENT F.D. Coy RE

| Place | Date | Hour | Summary of Events and Information | Remarks and references to Appendices |
|---|---|---|---|---|
| ENGLEBEMER | 1/6 | | | |
| BIVOUACS | | 0730 – ZERO : 2 day. Co. now affiliated to 87th Bde. | |
| | | 0820 | Forward reconnaissance officer (ii/t. A.F. TABRAHAM) +2.O.R. sent up to line to report to Bde. & then advance reconnoitred. | |
| | | 0930 | Company leaves Bivouacs & proceeds to line; on reporting to Bde. ordered to stand by. | |
| FRONT TRENCHES | | 0600 | Lt TABRAHAM ordered to return to Co. area. | |
| | | 0930 | Co. instructed by Bde. to stand by. | |
| | | | 1 man wounded slightly, evacuated. | |
| | | | Operations on this front stand still in considerable loss but no advance | ASR |
| | 2/7 | 1200 | Company rallies maintenance parties except that for front water supply were sent to Bivouacs @ ENGLEBEMER in accordance w/ Instructions from Bde. | |
| | | | 87th Bde. moved to HAMEL : HQ.: MESNIL. | |
| | | | On reporting to Bde. ordered to Stand by. | |
| | | | 1 O.R. seriously wounded subsequently died of wounds. | ASR |
| | 3/7 | | Co. ceases to be affiliated to 87th Bde. & becomes affiliated to 88th Bde. now belonging to Area – formerly Right Sector Dutnan Div Inst Divisional Front. | |
| | | | Work: Maintenance of tracks & tramways ; night wiring. (2.O. & 10 O.R.) | ASR |

# WAR DIARY
## or
## INTELLIGENCE SUMMARY.
(Erase heading not required.)

Army Form C. 2118.

| Place | Date | Hour | Summary of Events and Information | Remarks and references to Appendices |
|---|---|---|---|---|
| ENGLEBELMER | 1916. 3/7 | Morn. | During bombardment: (1) On bridge on the Doullens Road was damaged by shell fire & repaired | |
| | | | (2) A few slight repairs were rendered necessary on Tramway | OC/R |
| | | | (3) Tracks slightly damaged by shell hole | OC/R |
| | | | (4) No other damage at all done to Doul. Up & Down Roads, Tramways or Water System in Co. area. | OC/R |
| | | | (5) Englebelmer shelled intermittently but not severely. | OC/R |
| | 4/7 | | Work: Road repairs, maintenance. 10 R wounded (ankle) | |
| | 5/7 | | Work: Well sinking; wiring F. Right of Mary Redan, 30 yds of 91 OR, 130 x done 1 day; drawing & carrying fascines GABION AVENUE between METRE RAILWAY & ENGLE BELMER. | OC/R |
| | 6/7 | | 10.R. and 5. Hospital ; 2.O.R. wounded. | |
| | | | Work: Well sinking; wiring to R. of MARY REDAN, 500 x 2 rows of French wire complete; improving GABION AVENUE; theory Un Engrs O.P.; erecting Signal D/F Out. | OC/R |
| | 7/7 | | Snow (reinforcing draft) from Co. | OC/R |

Army Form C. 2118.

# WAR DIARY
## or
## INTELLIGENCE SUMMARY.
(Erase heading not required.)

| Place | Date | Hour | Summary of Events and Information | Remarks and references to Appendices |
|---|---|---|---|---|
| | 1916 | | | |
| ENGLE- | 7/7 | | 10.R. returned to duty from 29th Dual Reserve Bn. | |
| BELMER | | | 10.R. " " " " D. " C.R.E. Dump ... [illegible] ... [illegible] | |
| | | | 2.O.R. at present @ C.R.E. Dump proceed to ACHEUX for work at Div. WORKSHOPS & at PUMPING STATION respectively. | |
| | 8/7 | | Work: Well sinking; wiring to R. of MARY REDAN, 150ˣ done (one bay); improving GABION AVENUE; repairing VIII Corps O.P. Dug Out. | OS7/R |
| | | | 2.O.R. killed. | |
| | | | Work: Well sinking; wiring to R. of MARY REDAN, 120ˣ salliseau (1 bay) completed + 350ˣ one bay (complete; 3rd Bay of original entanglement) completed; improving GABION AVENUE; repairing VIII Corps O.P. Dug Out. | OS7/R |
| | 9/7 | | 10.R. admitted Hospital. | |
| | | | 10.R. returned to duty from Hospital. | |
| | | | Work: Well sinking; done repairing; improvement of GABION & WITHINGTON AVENUES; Revert to Corps O.P. | OS7/R |
| | 10/7 | | Work: as previous day; also wiring (no actual wiring done after stores taken to spot OS7/R to enemy shelling) | OS7/R |

# WAR DIARY
## INTELLIGENCE SUMMARY
*(Erase heading not required.)*

Army Form C. 2118.

Instructions regarding War Diaries and Intelligence Summaries are contained in F. S. Regs., Part II. and the Staff Manual respectively. Title pages will be prepared in manuscript.

| Place | Date | Hour | Summary of Events and Information | Remarks and references to Appendices |
|---|---|---|---|---|
| ENGLEBEL-MER | 1916 11/7 | | Work: Well sinking; road repairing; improvement of GABION & WITHINGTON AVENUES; drainage of ESSEX STREET; repairs to PATRICK'S AVENUE water pt.; wiring (120x 2 rows French Wire put out) | 007/R |
| | | | 10 O.R. Killed, 4 O.R. wounded (3 severely 1 slightly) | |
| | 12/7 | | Work: Well sinking; road repairing; improvement of GABION & WITHINGTON AVENUES; drainage & improvement of ESSEX STREET; repairs to Pipe Line & Water Points; wiring (2 addl. rows of French Wire put out whole length); making road from head cylinder to reservoir. | 007/R |
| | | | 2 O.R. admitted Hospital sick | |
| | 13/7 | | Work: Well sinking; road repairing; improvement of GABION & WITHINGTON AVENUE, s/f top of TIPPERARY AVENUE; improvement of ESSEX STREET; repairs to improvement of Water Points; VIII Corps O.P. | 003/R 003/R |
| | | | Strength of Coy.: 7 Offrs, 2 Interpreters, 186 O.R. | 004/R |
| | 14/7 15/7 | | Work: as previous day: TIPPERARY AVENUE work completed | |
| | | | Work: Well sinking; road & tramway repair; improvement of GABION & WITHINGTON AVENUES; improvement of ESSEX STREET; work started on Water Pt. & pipe line; VIII Corps O.P. | 007/R |
| | 16/7 | | 10 O.R. Returns from Hospital. 2 H.Q. forwarded section & transport arrived made & new line near FORCEVILLE ROAD | |

T2134. Wt. W708—776. 500000. 4/15. Sir J. C. & S.

# WAR DIARY
## INTELLIGENCE SUMMARY

Army Form C. 2118.

| Place | Date | Hour | Summary of Events and Information | Remarks and references to Appendices |
|---|---|---|---|---|
| ENGLEBEL-MER | 1916 | | | |
| | 6/7 | | Work: Well sinking; adjustment of front pump; road repairs; improvement of GABION & WITHINGTON AVENUES; improvement of ESSEX STREET & No 6 SAP; repairs to cylinders employed in FIRING LINE; Water post repairs; The bmps O.P. treatment of Dept Dept completed | O.J.R. |
| | 7/7 | | Works: Well sinking (about 16' "Damh"); road repairs; improvement of GABION & WITHINGTON AVENUES; improvement of No. 6 Sap & ESSEX STREET) water post repairs; Dep Dy Out to 1st Bde HQ. started muddy phone at Q 19 B 60.40 | O.J.R. |
| | 18/7 | | Works: Wellsinking; road repairs; improvement of WITHINGTON AVENUE; improvement ESSEX STREET; Water post repairs; Bde. HQ. Dep Dy O.E. | O.J.R. |
| | 19/7 | | Reinforcing draft of #114 join 6o + 2.O.R. return from hospital to 1.O.R. Routine from leave; 10.R. Wounded. | |
| | 20/7 | | Works: as previous day; also preparation of Tank + cub work thought for use in conjunction with Tank well in FORCEVILLE ROAD. 2.O.R. Adt to Hospital | O.J.R. |
| | | | Works: Well sinking; preparing timbers for cub for water Tank; improvement of WITHINGTON | |

# WAR DIARY

## WAR DIARY
## INTELLIGENCE SUMMARY.
(Erase heading not required.)

Army Form C. 2118.

Instructions regarding War Diaries and Intelligence Summaries are contained in F.S. Regs., Part II. and the Staff Manual respectively. Title pages will be prepared in manuscript.

| Place | Date | Hour | Summary of Events and Information | Remarks and references to Appendices |
|---|---|---|---|---|
| ENGLEBEL-MER | 1916 | | AVENUE; improvement of ESSEX STREET; Water first repairs; village water supply repairs; Bde H.Q. Dug Outs; road repairs. Went round trenches & C.R.E., T.R.E. | |
| | 21/7 | | I.O.R. attd. to C.R.E. for duty. Work: Dillworthy, preparing site for Tank + trench for pipe line; repairing damage to deep dugouts; improving WITHINGTON AVENUE; work on Bde Office hut; assisting infantry front line in revetting; preparing to lay new pipe line along 1st AVENUE, compelling repairs to St PATRICKS AVENUE new water first, petrolling pipeline from AUCHONVILLERS to 2nd AVENUE; marking out new communication trench from MARYLEBONE ROAD; Bde HQ Dug Outs. | OO/R |
| | | | 1 Lieut. HIGGINS + 1 Lieut BOYCE join Co.<br>1 O.R. wounded.<br>2 O.R. sick to Hospital | OO/R |
| | 22/7 | | William Company moved out of Billets in ENGLEBELMER to Camp on S.W. of village close to ENGLEBELMER – FORCEVILLE cross country waggon Road.<br>Work: Erecting shelters + preparing Camp; work in connection with new Well, tank + pipe line; repairing damage to deep dug outs; work in Bde office hut + Bde. Dy Out; front line revetting; preparing for new pipeline along 1st AVENUE; work on new Bde HQ Dugout. | |

# WAR DIARY
## INTELLIGENCE SUMMARY.
*(Erase heading not required.)*

Army Form C. 2118.

| Place | Date | Hour | Summary of Events and Information | Remarks and references to Appendices |
|---|---|---|---|---|
| ENGLEBEL- | 1916 22/7 | | Improving wiring in front of new fire trench to R. of MARY REDAN. | |
| MER | | | C.R.E. Conference: informed that Co was to move out of dets shortly. | OO/R |
| | 23/7 | | Lt RITCHING rejoins Co. | |
| | | | 2.O.R. return from attachment C.R.E. | |
| | | | 1.O.R. returns from Hospital. | |
| | | | Work: Erecting shelters at new Camp; work on newdell Pipeline; repairs to deep dugouts; Front line revetting; road repairs; work on new pipeline along 1st AVENUE. | |
| | | | Went round Co area with Officer Commanding Co. | OO/R |
| | 24/7 | | Lt. STEPHEN joins Co.   1.O.R. sick to Hospital. | |
| | | 0200 | In accordance with orders Co moves from ENGLEBELMER | OO/R |
| | 25/7 | 0500 | Company arrives at LOUVEN COURT & goes into BIVOUACS there | OO/R |
| | | | Strength of Co. 11 Offrs, 1 Industfus, + 198 (excluding 2 attd A.O., 3 attd C.R.E., 1 w.C.E., 1 W. Beaucourt) | OO/R |
| | | | 1.O.R. sick to Hospital. | |
| | | | 2.O.R. rejoin Co. from C.R.E. | |
| | 26/7 | | Work: parade, inspections, fatigues. | OO/R |
| | | | 3.O.R. rejoin Co. from Hospital. 1.O.R. joins Co as reinforcement. | OO/R |

# WAR DIARY
## INTELLIGENCE SUMMARY

Army Form C. 2118.

| Place | Date | Hour | Summary of Events and Information | Remarks and references to Appendices |
|---|---|---|---|---|
| LOUVENCOURT | 1916 | | | |
| | 26/7 | | Work: Parade, drill, fatigues | Coy R |
| | 27/7 | 1700 | Company marched to DOULLENS and entrained for PROVEN. 2 O.R. rejoin from Bde S.O. | Coy R |
| | 28/7 | 0019 | Drew rations for PROVEN via HAZEBROUCK. 1 O.R. Driver Wagon on Advd Rations | |
| | | 0809 | Arrive @ PROVEN | |
| | 29/7 | | Proceed via POPERINGHE to MWW quarries at H.7.a.39. 30 cwt lorries being used. A 28 cwt | Coy R |
| | | | 1 O.R. sick to Hospital. | |
| | | | 2 O.R. again attached S.O. of Bde. | Coy R |
| | | | 1 driver All. with Wagon three rejoins train | Coy R |
| | 30/7 | | Went round front lines with O.C. 172nd Coy R.E. with a view to taking over | Coy R |
| | | | 1 O.R. returns to duty from Hospital | |
| | | | Bivouacs | |
| | 31/7 | | R.E. stores taken over from 12" Feet R.E. | W.J. |
| | | | One section sent up to forward billets in YPRES. | |

W Jogan Capt.
for O.C. 173rd Kent Field Coy R.E.

29th Divisional Engineers

-----

1/3rd KENT

FEILD COMPANY RE.

AUGUST 1 9 1 6

1/3 Kent Field Coy R.E (T)

Army Form C. 2118.

# WAR DIARY
## or
## INTELLIGENCE SUMMARY.
(Erase heading not required.)

Vol 6

| Place | Date | Hour | Summary of Events and Information | Remarks and references to Appendices |
|---|---|---|---|---|
| H.T.A.29. | 1/6/16 | — | 25/ 6 O.R. 196 G.R.E. + 2 O.R. + 33 hours Inn Bridge Train Sch. att. for ration | — |
| | | | Lt. L.C. Hall — To Second Army School. | W.J. |
| | 2/6/16 | — | 10.R. return to duty. | |
| | 3/6/16 | — | 10.R. to Record Army School. 10.R. sick to hospital. | W.J. |
| | | | M. Sheen (interalia) Return to French tenure. | W.J. |
| | 4/6/16 | — | 10.R. att. to CRE for duty & rations. | W.J. |
| | | | 10.R. C.A. to Corps Park R.E. for duty & rations. | W.J. |
| | 5/6/16 | — | — | |
| | 6/6/16 | — | 10.R. returned to duty from hospital | W.J. |
| | 7/6/16 | — | No 3 section proceeded to forward billet. | W.J. |
| W.J. | 7/6/16 | — | — | |
| | 8/6/16 | — | 48 O.R att. for drainage work. | W.J. |
| | 9/6/16 | — | 10.R. att. (Hants Regt) slightly poisd. admit. hospital. | W.J. |
| | | | 2 O.R. att. (Essex Regt) admit. hospital wounded. | W.J. |

1/3 Kent Field Co R E (T)

# WAR DIARY
## or
## INTELLIGENCE SUMMARY.
(Erase heading not required.)

Army Form C. 2118.

Instructions regarding War Diaries and Intelligence Summaries are contained in F. S. Regs., Part II. and the Staff Manual respectively. Title pages will be prepared in manuscript.

| Place | Date | Hour | Summary of Events and Information | Remarks and references to Appendices |
|---|---|---|---|---|
| H7n.29 | 10/5/16 | — | 1 O.R. ad. Wounded admit Hosp | W.J |
| | 11/5/16 | — | | W.J |
| | 12/5/16 | | 13 O.R. att 86 Bde for ration & duty | W.J |
| | 13/5/16 | | (2) O.R. (R.A.M.C.) att for work in yard | W.J |
| | | | 1 O.R. admit Hosp | |
| | 14/5/16 | | 25 O.R. 196 Co Re arrived to be att for relief | W.J |
| | 15/5/16 | | 3 O.R. au Div. School for training | W.J |
| | 16/5/16 | | | W.J |
| | 17/5/16 | | 3 O.R. (Reinforcement) joined | W.J |
| | | | 2 O.R. admit Hosp | |
| | | | 1 O.R. att adm'd Hosp | |
| | 18/5/16 | | 1 O.R. admit Hosp | W.J |
| | | | 1 O.R. return to duty from Hosp | |
| | | | 2 O.R. att admit Hosp | |
| | 19/5/16 | | 1 O.R. att admit Hosp | W.J |
| | | | 1 O.R. return to duty | |
| | 26/5/16 | | 1 O.R. att for drainage work admitted Hosp (sick) | G.J.R |

1/3 Kent Field Co R.E.(T)

Army Form C. 2118.

# WAR DIARY
## INTELLIGENCE SUMMARY.
(Erase heading not required.)

| Place | Date | Hour | Summary of Events and Information | Remarks and references to Appendices |
|---|---|---|---|---|
| | 1916 | | | |
| H 7a 29 | 20/8 | | Section returns to Somerset killed relieving section 2 | A/JR |
| | 21/8 | | 2.O.R. 2nd Bridging Train attached | A/JR |
| | | | 1.O.R. returned to duty from Hosp. | A/JR |
| | 22/8 | | 1.O.R. attached for rations & duty (RAMC) | A/JR |
| | 23/8 | | — | A/JR |
| | 24/8 | | 1.O.R. admitted hospital (deaf) | A/JR |
| | | | 1.O.R. attached for drainage work admitted Hosp.(sick) | |
| | 25/8 | | 1.O.R. returned to duty fr. hospital | |
| | | | 1.O.R. att'd for drainage returns to duty from Hospital | |
| | | | 1.O.R. alt " " proceeds on leave | |
| | | | 1.O.R. " " admitted Hosp.(sick) | A/JR |
| | 26/8 | | 1.O.R. proceeds to ENGLAND on leave | |
| | | | 1.NCO & 9 men (RAMC; yard party) changed for an equal number of NCO's & men | A/JR |
| | | | 2.O.R. att'd for drainage reported missing | |
| | 27/8 | | — | |
| | 28/8 | | 1.O.R. adm't Hosp. 2nd Cpl. Marshall | |

1/3 Kent Field Amb (T)

Army Form C. 2118.

# WAR DIARY
## or
## INTELLIGENCE SUMMARY.
*(Erase heading not required.)*

Instructions regarding War Diaries and Intelligence Summaries are contained in F.S. Regs, Part II. and the Staff Manual respectively. Title pages will be prepared in manuscript.

| Place | Date | Hour | Summary of Events and Information | Remarks and references to Appendices |
|---|---|---|---|---|
| | 1916 | | | |
| H.7.a.2.9 | 28/6 | | 1 O.R. return from leave. | W.7 |
| | 29/6 | | Lt. Hall & return when from 2nd Army Central Training School. S/o 87 Bde A.S.C. | W.7. |
| | 30/6 | | 1 O.R. return to duty from dental treatment. 1 relieves temporary L/C. | |
| | 3/5 | | C.S.M. Harding admit. Hosp. for dental treatment. 1 O.R. admit. Hosp. | |

S Tyson Capt RE
for OC 1/3rd Kent field Amb RE

29th Divisional Engineers
--------------------------------

1/3rd KENT

FIELD COMPANY R. E.

SEPTEMBER 1 9 1 6

1/3 Kent Field Co RE. TF.

Army Form C. 2118.

Vol 7

# WAR DIARY
## or
## INTELLIGENCE SUMMARY.
*(Erase heading not required.)*

| Place | Date | Hour | Summary of Events and Information | Remarks and references to Appendices |
|---|---|---|---|---|
| H7A&9 | 1/9/16 | — | | |
| | 2/9. | | 1. O.R. Proceed to ENGLAND on leave | W. |
| | | | 1.O.R. to Hosp. (Sick) Hosp. | W. |
| | 3/9 | | 1.O.R. Returned from Hosp. | |
| | | | 3 N.C.O.s Return to duty from Sid. School. | |
| | | | 1 OR att return to duty from Hosp | |
| | | | No. 3 Section Proceeded to YPRES & relieved No 4. | W. |
| | 4/9. | | 1 OR Returns to duty from leave. | W. |
| | 5/9. | | 1.O.R. att Div. Schl. as RE Instructor. | W. |
| | | | 1 RAMC admit. Hosp. | W. |
| | 6/9 | | 2 OR join'd Coy from 2 Terr. Base Depot | |
| | 7/9. | | 1 OR Killed. | |
| | | | 10 R wounded. | |
| | | | 1s R Sick to Hosp. | W. |
| | 8/9. | | Sapper Smith # 1682 aO. C.R.E. | |
| | | | 1. O R Sick to Hosp. | W. |

1/3 Kent Field Cd R.E. T.F.

Army Form C. 2118.

# WAR DIARY
## or
## INTELLIGENCE SUMMARY.
(Erase heading not required.)

| Place | Date | Hour | Summary of Events and Information | Remarks and references to Appendices |
|---|---|---|---|---|
| | 1916 | | | |
| H.7.A.2.9. | 9/9 | — | 1 oR Sid to Hosp. No 4 Sectri Steam No 1 at Forward hill | WB |
| | 10/9 | | 1 oR Rej to Hosp. | WB |
| | 11/9 | | 19 oR R.A.M.C. return to Unit. | WB |
| | 12/9 | | Divin Hy.den Refuels at Popienghe with Spring cart Suppls. R.E. Complete to die under | WB |
| | | | 1 oR join unit | |
| | | | 36 oR 2 came off duty. crew to be at [?] for returning Sp | WB |
| | 13/9 | | 32 oR Sd up Posh at 7pm returning to work | WB |
| | 14/9 | | Sapper Foster 2542 transferred to Base | WB |
| | 15/9 | | 2 oR att cohort Hosp. | WB |
| | 16/9 | | 1 oR return from Leave. | WB |
| | 17/9 | | No 1 Sectrin Steam No 2 at Forward hill. | WB |
| | | | 1st KITCHING + 29 men fd to ST JEAN TER BIEZEN for special work under C.E. VII Corps | OJR |

1/3 Kent Field Coy R.E. T.F.

Army Form C. 2118

# WAR DIARY
## or
## INTELLIGENCE SUMMARY
(Erase heading not required.)

Instructions regarding War Diaries and Intelligence Summaries are contained in F. S. Regs., Part II. and the Staff Manual respectively. Title Pages will be prepared in manuscript.

| Place | Date | Hour | Summary of Events and Information | Remarks and references to Appendices |
|---|---|---|---|---|
|  | 1916 |  |  |  |
| H 7 a 29.18.19 |  |  | Lt. W. STEPHEN wounded (shell) @ JUNCTION TRENCH (I 11 d 9 5) + evacuated to 10th C.C.S.; 1 O.R. (stoker) to 10th C.C.S. |  |
|  |  |  | 1 O.R. to join Lt. KITCHING'S party. |  |
|  |  |  | Attached personnel from 5th Bde: 2 killed, 1 wounded, 1 sick to hospital |  |
|  |  |  | 4 O.R. reinforcement to Co. |  |
|  |  |  | 1 O.R. attached to duty | 003/R |
|  | 19/9 |  | Nil | 003/R |
|  | 20/9 |  | 2nd Lt. W.H. NEVELL joins company as reinforcement. | 003/R |
|  | 21/9 |  | — | 003/R |
|  | 22/9 |  | 1 O.R. returns to duty | 003/R |
|  | 23/9 |  | — | 003/R |
|  | 24/9 |  | 1 O.R. (Pioneer) attd admitted Hosp. | 004/R |
|  | 25/9 |  | 2 O.R. reinforcing draft join Co. | 003/R |
|  | 26/9 |  | Lt. HALL & Lt. HUGGINS & 12 O.R. attd FRAN'S HORSE 2nd ANZAC CORPS. | 003/R |
|  | 27/9 |  | 1 O.R. returns to duty | 003/R |
|  | 28/9 |  | — | 003/R |

1/3 Kent Field Co R.E.

Army Form C. 2118

# WAR DIARY
# or
# INTELLIGENCE SUMMARY
(Erase heading not required.)

| Place | Date | Hour | Summary of Events and Information | Remarks and references to Appendices |
|---|---|---|---|---|
| | 19/6 | | 10.R. admitted Hosp. | OC/R |
| H7a 2.9 | 29/9 | | 30.R. Transferred to "Base unfit for A.S. in the Fd." | OC/R |
| | 30/9 | | | OC/R |
| | | | Note: Ommission for 6/8/16 : 10R att'd CRE | OC/R |

OC/R Ruston
Major R.E.(T)
O.C. 1/3 Kent Field Co. R.E.

29th Divisional Engineers

------

1/3rd KENT FIELD COMPANY R. E.

OCTOBER 1 9 1 6

# WAR DIARY
## INTELLIGENCE SUMMARY
*(Erase heading not required.)*

Army Form C. 2118

1/3 Kent Fd Coy
J.C.8

| Place | Date 1916 | Hour | Summary of Events and Information | Remarks and references to Appendices |
|---|---|---|---|---|
| Hyc 29 | 1/10 | | Section 3 returns detachment of Section 4 in forward Billets | copy/R |
| BRADNOR | 2/10 | | 1 O.R. Admitted Hosp. sick | copy/R |
| | 3/10 | | 1 O.R. to Hosp. injured | |
| | | | 1 O.R. return to duty from C.R.E. | |
| | | | Order recd to move to HOUTKERQUE on 4th | |
| | | | Forward party moved to Back Billets leaving small body in over party behind | copy/R |
| | 4/10 | | Moved forward to 5th | |
| | 5/10 | | Advance party of 2 Wessex Field Co. (2/1st WEST LANCS.) arrived & took over BACK BILLETS | copy/R |
| | | | Advance party of 2 Wessex Field Co. to take over FORWARD BILLETS & work | copy/R |
| HOUTKERQUE | | | Co. moved to HOUTKERQUE being those joined by Section detached @ ST JEAN TER | |
| | | | | T.I.O.R. returning & leave | copy/R |
| BRADNOR | 4/10 | | 1 Lt. A.L. BOYCE & one other rank proved as Advance Party via POPERINGHE to ALLONVILLE x | copy/R |
| HOUTKERQUE | 6/10 | | 1 Lt. T. BURKLEY proceeds to leave | copy/R |
| | | | 29 R dl R.E. instituted by A.O.C. via Etaples | |
| EN ROUTE | 7/10 | | Co. proceeds to PROVEN & entrain for SALEUX | copy/R |
| do | 8/10 | | Co. detrain @ SALEUX & marche to | copy/R |
| ALLONVILLE | | | ALLONVILLE being joined by 1st Lt. BOYCE & 1 O.R. advance party. { 5 Offr D.S.O.R (not rtg) 7 of Rank & 2 Ascheros atd | copy/R |
| do | 9/10 | | 2 O.R. admitted hospital sick | copy/R |

# WAR DIARY
## INTELLIGENCE SUMMARY

*(Erase heading not required.)*

Army Form C. 2118

| Place | Date | Hour | Summary of Events and Information | Remarks and references to Appendices |
|---|---|---|---|---|
| ALLONVILLE | 1916 9/10 | | 10.R. returned from leave. | |
| do | 10/10 | 10.45 am | 10 Offs. & 5 O.R. proceed to BUIRE as billeting party | O57/R |
| do | | 3.45 pm | Coy marches to BUIRE | |
| BUIRE | | 8.45 pm | Company arrives at BUIRE | O59/R |
| do | 11/10 | | 10.R. stores rec billets, being signed by billeting party | |
| | | | 10.R. admitted Hospital (sick) | |
| do | 12/10 | | 10.R. (Cyclist Orderly) attached C.R.E. | O57/R |
| | | | O.R. Benjamin Co. transferred to 56th Bde. & 87th Bde. | O57/R |
| do | 13/10 | | 10.R. returns to duty from Hosp. 10.R. trans. to 2 Bde. | O59/R |
| | | 10.30 am | Co. marches to MAMETZ WOOD in 86 Bde. | |
| MAMETZ WOOD | 14/10 | 4.30 pm | Co. arrive @ | O57/R |
| do | | | 1.O.R. accidentally injured admt. Hospital | O57/R |
| | 15/10 | | Co. attached for work to XV Corps Troops except details kept in Camp for Divn work | O59/R |
| | 15/10 | | 1 O.R. struck off duty from Hospital | O59/R |
| | 16/10 | | Mashrump – | O59/R |
| | 17/10 | | 2 detms returned on duty fr. XV Corps | |
| | 18/10 | | 2 " start work to a'r making for Divn. | |
| | | | 10.R. Left for U.K. | O59/R |
| | | | 10.R. admitted Hosp. sick | O57/R |

# WAR DIARY
## INTELLIGENCE SUMMARY
*(Erase heading not required.)*

Army Form C. 2118

| Place | Date | Hour | Summary of Events and Information | Remarks and references to Appendices |
|---|---|---|---|---|
| MAMETZ WOOD | 18/10 | | Returns Rutty, 2 returns road making. | OO4/R |
| | 19/10 | | 10.R. admitted Hosp. Sick. | |
| | | | 10.R. returns to duty. | OO4/R |
| do | | | Work as previous day | |
| do | 20/10 | | Bo. moves to | |
| BERNAFAY WOOD CAMP | | | BERNAFAY WOOD CAMP (S 28 & 37.) | OO4/R |
| | 21/10 | | 30.R. reinforcements join Co. | OO4/R |
| | 22/10 | | 3.O.R. admitted Hospital Sick. | OO4/R |
| | 23/10 | | 1.O.R. admitted Hospital Sick | OO4/R |
| | | | 1.O.R. " wounded. | OO4/R |
| | | | 1 animal wounded taken away. | |
| | | | 1.O.R. proceeds on leave. | |
| | 24/10 | | Left BERNAFAY WOOD CAMP & moved to another Camp on BERNAFAY WOOD - LONGUEVAL ROAD | OO4/R |
| S 23 a 48 | | | at S.23.a.48 | |
| | 25/10 | | 10.R. sick to Hospital | OO4/R |
| | 26/10 | | 2O.R. " " " | 104/R |
| | 27/10 | | 4.O.R. return to duty from Hospital. | OO4/R |
| | | | — | OO4/R |

# WAR DIARY

## INTELLIGENCE SUMMARY

*(Erase heading not required.)*

Army Form C. 2118

Instructions regarding War Diaries and Intelligence Summaries are contained in F. S. Regs., Part II. and the Staff Manual respectively. Title Pages will be prepared in manuscript.

| Place | Date 1916 | Hour | Summary of Events and Information | Remarks and references to Appendices |
|---|---|---|---|---|
| S 23 a.8 | 28/10 | | 1 O.R. att'd C.R.E. | OC/R |
| | 29/10 | | — | OC/R |
| | 30/10 | | 1 O.R. rtn'd to duty from Hospital. Company marched to 526 Central on relief by 1st Aust. Fld. Co. | OC/R |
| S 26 Cent | 31/10 | | 6 O.R. rejoined from C.R.E. — | OC/R |

OC/R Norton
Major R.E.(T)
O.C. 1/3rd Wessex R.E.

3 R.G. "Networks"

S E C R E T.
\*\*\*\*\*\*\*\*\*\*\*

Copy No. 4

C.R.E's. Order No.23.

Refce: 1/40,000 Albert combined sheet.   29th October, 1916.
1/20,000 France. Sheet 57 C S.W.

The following orders are extracted from 29th Division Order No. 72 dated 28th October, 1916.

1. The 29th Division will be relieved in the line by the 1st Australian Division on the night of the 29th/30th October.

2. Moves will be carried out in accordance with the attached movement tables on the 30th October.

3. Details of handing over will be arranged between Companies. Pontoons of incoming and outgoing Companies will be exchanged to save their transport if considered desirable.

4. Units on relief will hand over to the incoming units all secret trench maps and instructions, and the secret Operation Orders issued.

5. All Camps are to be left standing, and government property in the shape of tents, tarpaulins, tables, chairs, &c. is on no account to be removed from them. All Camps will be taken over by advanced Parties, and handed over by rear parties, especially detailed for this purpose. The allotment of accommodation in a Camp will be carried out by the Brigade, whose Headquarters are situated in that Camp.

6. Completion of all reliefs will be reported to the C. R. E.

7. The C.R.E., 29th Division will hand over to the C.R.E., 1st Australian Division on October 30th. Headquarters R.E. will close at POMMIERS REDOUBT and open at BELLEVUE FARM, E.5.c. on the same day.

8. Acknowledge by wire.

Issued at   0950

B Thillon

Captain R.E.,
Adjutant R.E., 29th Division.

Copy No.1   C.R.E., 29th Division.
2   West Riding Field Co., R.E.
3   London Field Co. R.E.
4   Kent Field Co., R.E.
5   C.R.E., 1st Australian Division.

## Movement of Field Companies.

| | Positions on 29th Oct. | March on 30th to | Route. |
|---|---|---|---|
| 1/2nd London Field Co., R.E. | S.28.b.3.2. | POMMIERS CAMP | MONTAUBAN. |
| 1/3rd Kent Field Co., R.E. | S.23.a.4.7. | MAMETZ. | MONTAUBAN. |
| 1/1st West Riding Field Co., R.E. | S.23.a.4.5. | KRICOURT. | MONTAUBAN. |

Troops on the march will maintain 200 yards between companies.

Bethlen / Capt R E

29th Division

------

1/3rd KENT FIELD COMPANY R. E.

NOVEMBER 1 9 1 6

Army Form C. 2118

# WAR DIARY
## INTELLIGENCE SUMMARY

1/3rd Kent & with the R.E. (T)

(Erase heading not required.)

Instructions regarding War Diaries and Intelligence Summaries are contained in F. S. Regs., Part II. and the Staff Manual respectively. Title Pages will be prepared in manuscript.

| Place | Date 1916 | Hour | Summary of Events and Information | Remarks and references to Appendices |
|---|---|---|---|---|
| 52b.Cent. | 1/11 | | Company moved into billets at CORBIE | |
| CORBIE | | | Strength of Company: | |
| | | | Officers 9 O.R. 209 O.R. (including 1st Nevell) | O.C.4/R |
| | | | Return Strength 9 Offrs + 193 O.R. (including 1 Lt Buckley (att) but excluding 17 NEVELL on leave) | O.C.4/R |
| | 2/11 | | 1 O.R. Transferred to Base (umbrage) Authority D.A.G. AY 2467 | O.C.4/R |
| | 3/11 | | 1 O.R. admitted hospital. Interpreter joins Co. | O.C.4/R |
| | 4/11 | | 1 O.R. admitted hospital | O.C.4/R |
| | 5/11 | | — | |
| | 6/11 | | 1 O.R. admitted hospital | O.C.4/R |
| | 7/11 | | 1 O.R. | O.C.4/R |
| | 8/11 | | 1 Lt G. AN KITCHING, between times, attached C.R.E. (Offrs & out no Cast.Coy r) | O.C.4/R |
| | | | 1 Lt. AT. BOYCE proceeds on leave to HAVRE. | |
| | 9/11 | | — | O.C.4/R |
| | 10/11 | | — | O.C.4/R |
| | 11/11 | | 1 O.R. admitted hospital (sick) | O.C.4/R |
| | | | 1 O.R. Transferred Base | |
| MÉAULTE | 12/11 | | Co. Hdqrs & 1 Section transport move to billets in MÉAULTE | O.C.4/R |
| | | | × 1 Officer (1st Lt E. HUGGINS) + 36 O.R. — officers - 4 O.R. — drivers — | O.C.4/R |
| SANDPITS CAMP E.24.a Cent. | 13/11 | | Co. also 1 section transport moves into Camp at E.24.a Central | O.C.4/R |

1875 Wt. W593/826 1,000,000 4/15 J.B.C. & A. A.D.S.S./Forms/C. 2118.

# WAR DIARY
## INTELLIGENCE SUMMARY

*(Erase heading not required.)*

Army Form C. 2118

| Place | Date 1916 | Hour | Summary of Events and Information | Remarks and references to Appendices |
|---|---|---|---|---|
| SAND PITS CAMP | 14/11 | | 2/Lt. W.J TURNER admitted Hospital sick. 1 O.R. (Batman) accompanies 2/Lt. TURNER. 3.O.R. admitted Hospital sick. | |
| | 15/11 | | 2/Lt. A.C. BOYCE returns to duty from leave. 3.O.R. admitted Hospital sick. 1 O.R. w. 2 horses returns to detached Section at CORBIE | 027/R |
| | 16/11 | | 10 O.R. posted to S29 c.32 as advance party to take over from 2nd Company which is to be Relieved. 3.O.R. reinforcements (2 N.C.O. + 1 Dvr) join Section at CORBIE. 10.R. (officers batman) returns to duty from Hospital. | 027/R |
| | 17/11 | | 2/Offr (2/Lt. E.G. HUGGINS) + 44 O.R. ranks rejoin B. from CORBIE. 5.O.R. admitted Hospital sick. | 027/R |
| BERNAFAY WOOD S 29 c 32 | | | Co. moves to Documental Personnel to S 29 c.32. 2 cars to Transport + Mounted Personnel to A3 B08. H.Q. @ S29.C.32 N.E. corner of BERNAFAY WOOD. 2.O.R. Sanitary Section attached to Coy. for returns as from 19/11 | 027/R |
| | 18/11 19/11 | | ---10.R. returns to duty from Hospital. A 6 R. admitted Hospital | 027/R |
| | 20/11 | | 1 2.O.R. (Battery Ruins Park) attached for rations co from 22/11 2/L.. H.D. "Hinds" do do " forage no " " 22/11 | 027/R |
| | 21/11 | | 1 N.C.O. (1st Cavalry Reserve Park) attached for rations do from 23/11 2.O.R. admitted Hospital. | 027/R |

# WAR DIARY
## or
## INTELLIGENCE SUMMARY

*(Erase heading not required.)*

Army Form C. 2118

| Place | Date 1916 | Hour | Summary of Events and Information | Remarks and references to Appendices |
|---|---|---|---|---|
| BERNAFAY WOOD S29 C 3.2 | 22/11 | | A.O.R. admitted Hospital. | OO4/R |
| | 23/11 | | 10.R. (1st Reserve Cavalry Park) admitted Hospital. 1 Sheep & Carriage Annext (1st Reserve Car. Park) attached for rations | OO4/R |
| | 24/11 | | 10.R. admitted Hospital. | OO4/R |
| | 25/11 | | 20.R. return to duty. Lt. A.F.TABRAHAM Transferred to R.F.C. | OO4/R |
| | 26/11 | | 20.R. admitted Hospital. 10.R. (1st Cavalry Reserve Park) Admitted Hospital. | OO4/R OO4/R |
| | 26/11 | | 10.R. returned to duty from Hospital. | OO4/R |
| | 26/11 | | 50.R. returned to duty from Hospital. 14 O.R. went to install Camp fireworks. | OO4/R |
| | 27/11 | | 10.R. admitted hospital. | OO4/R |
| | 28/11 | | 10.R. returns from leave. 10.R. returns to duty from Hospital | OO4/R |
| | 29/11 | | — | |
| | 29/11 | | 10.R. admitted Hospital. 10.R. proceeds on leave. | OO4/R |
| | 30/11 | | 2.O.R. admitted Hosp. (1 Anck) 20.R. ret to duty from Hospital. 6 O.R. reinforcements from Co. | OO4/R |

OO4/R noter  Major R.E.(T.)
O.E. 1/3rd Kent Fld. Co. R.E.

29th Divisional Engineers

------

1/3rd KENT FIELD COMPANY R. E.

DECEMBER 1 9 1 6

## Confidential

# War Diary

of

1/3rd Kent Field Coy. R.E.(T)

from December 1st 1916 to December 31st 1916

(Volume 1)

# WAR DIARY or INTELLIGENCE SUMMARY

Army Form C. 2118

*(Erase heading not required.)*

| Place | Date 1916 | Hour | Summary of Events and Information | Remarks and references to Appendices |
|---|---|---|---|---|
| BERNAFAY WOOD S29c32 | 1/12 | | Effective strength of Co. 8 Offrs, 1 Enlist, 1207 O.R. | OC4/R |
| | | | 10 R (attached) admitted 1 Offr. sick | OC4/R |
| | 2/12 | | 10 R. admitted Hospital Sick. | OC4/R |
| | 3/12 | | 20 R. proceed on Leave | |
| | 4/12 | | 10 R. proceed on Leave. | OC4/R |
| | | | 10 R admitted Hospital Sick | |
| | 5/12 | | 10 R. proceed on Leave. 10 R. return to duty from hospital | OC4/R |
| | 6/12 | | 20 R. proceed on Leave. | OC4/R |
| | 7/12 | | 10 R. " | OC4/R |
| | | | 10 R. admitted Hosp. Sick. | OC4/R |
| | 8/12 | | 60 R. reinforcements from Base. | OC4/R |
| | | | 10 R. reports from Hospital | OC4/R |
| | | | 10 R transferred to Base. | OC4/R |
| | 9/12 | | 10 R. proceeds on leave | OC4/R |
| | 10/12 | | 20 R proceed on leave. | OC4/R |
| | | | 1 R admitted Hospital | |
| | | | 10 R returns to duty. | |
| MANSEL CAMP | 11/12 | | 10 R. proceeds on leave. | OC4/R |
| | | | Co. moves to MANSEL CAMP | OC4/R |

# WAR DIARY or INTELLIGENCE SUMMARY

Army Form C. 2118

| Place | Date 1916 | Hour | Summary of Events and Information | Remarks and references to Appendices |
|---|---|---|---|---|
| MANSEL CAMP | 12/12 | | Company moves to billets at | 027R |
| MEAULTE | 13/12 | | MEAULTE.<br>1 O.R. proceeds on leave.<br>2 O.R. return to duty from Hospital.<br>1 Officer joins Company.<br>Company (less 1 Section consist of 1 Offr, 36 O.R. dismounted, 9 O.R. mounted with 17 animals) moves to PECQUIGNY. (Rifles by train CHANGEST + Transport by ROAD. | 027R |
| PECQUIGNY & CORBIE | 14/12 | | D.M. Section of Co. arrive at PECQUIGNY.<br>TRANSPORT arrives @ CORBIE.<br>1 O.R. admitted Hospital.<br>2 O.R. return to duty from Hospital.<br>Transport proceeds to arrives @ PECQUIGNY | 027R<br>027R |
| PECQUIGNY | 15/12 | | 1 O.R. rank (reinforcement) joins Co. | 027R |
| | 16/12 | | 1 O.R. returns to duty from Hosp. | 027R |
| | 17/12 | | 1 O.R. returns to duty from Hosp. | 027R |

Army Form C. 2118

# WAR DIARY
## INTELLIGENCE SUMMARY
*(Erase heading not required.)*

Instructions regarding War Diaries and Intelligence Summaries are contained in F.S. Regs., Part II. and the Staff Manual respectively. Title Pages will be prepared in manuscript.

| Place | Date | Hour | Summary of Events and Information | Remarks and references to Appendices |
|---|---|---|---|---|
| RECQUIGNY | 18/12 | | 2.O.R. return to duty from leave | O.o/R |
| do | 19/12 | | — | O.o/R |
| do | 20/12 | | 2.O.R. return from leave. | O.o/R |
| | | | 1.O.R. returned from hospital | O.o/R |
| do. | 21/12 | | — | O.o/R |
| do | 22/12 | | 1.O.R. return from leave. | O.o/R |
| | | | 1.O.R. goes on leave. | |
| do | 23/12 | | 1.O.R. transferred to base | O.o/R |
| | | | 1 Officer rejoins from base (2Lt. W.H. NEVELL) | |
| do | 24/12 | | 2 Officers proceed on leave (R.4th.R.R.J. MORGAN 2Lt. L.C. HALL) | |
| | | | 1.O.R. proceeds on leave | |
| | | | 2.O.R. return from leave | |
| do | 25/12 | | 1.O.R. (MEAULTE Det.) admitted hosp. ank. | O.o/R |
| do | 26/12 | | 3.O.R. return from leave | O.o/R |
| do | 27/12 | | 1.O.R. proceeds to Divl. Gas School for Course. | O.o/R |
| do. | 28/12 | | 2.O.R. return from leave. | do. |
| | | | 1.O.R. proceeds on leave | do. |
| do. | 29/12 | | 1.O.R. proceeds on leave. | do. |

# WAR DIARY
## or
## INTELLIGENCE SUMMARY
*(Erase heading not required.)*

Army Form C. 2118

Instructions regarding War Diaries and Intelligence Summaries are contained in F. S. Regs., Part II. and the Staff Manual respectively. Title Pages will be prepared in manuscript.

| Place | Date | Hour | Summary of Events and Information | Remarks and references to Appendices |
|---|---|---|---|---|
| Poperinghe | 29/12 | | 2. O.R. admitted to Hospital sick. | M |
| | | | 6. O.R. join Company. | |
| | 30/12 | | 1. O.R. (Gunnults Pindp) admitted hospital sick. | M |
| | | | 1. O.R. proceeded on leave. | M |
| | 31/12 | | 1. Officer proceeded on leave. (Major A.J.G. Renshaw). | |
| | | | 1. Officer returns from leave. (Capt. R.R.J. Morgan). | |
| | | | 1. Officer proceeded on leave. (1st Lieut. B.G. Huggins). | |

J. Schmitt
1st Lieut. R.E. (T).
A/O.C. 1/3 Kent Field Coy. R.E.
1/1/17.

WAR DIARY

OF

1/3rd KENT FIELD CO., R.E.

for month of
JANUARY 1917.

VOLUME XVI

# WAR DIARY or INTELLIGENCE SUMMARY

Army Form C. 2118

| Place | Date | Hour | Summary of Events and Information | Remarks and references to Appendices |
|---|---|---|---|---|
| Peppegny | 1/1/17 | | 1.O.R. proceeds on leave. | Nil. |
| " | 2/1/17 | | 1.O.R. proceeds on leave. 1 1.O.R. returns to duty from hospital. | |
| | | | 1 Officer proceeded on leave of Indication at L. Panry. (Capt. 1? R.J. Morgan). | Nil. |
| | | | 1.O.R. admitted to hospital sick. (Neuilli-Paris). | |
| | 3/1/17 | | 1.O.R. proceeds on leave. | Nil. |
| | | | 1.O.R. Course of Instruction. (Dept. Ford). | Nil. |
| | | | 2.O.R. proceed for from Base. | Nil. |
| | 4/1/17 | | 2.O.R. proceeded on leave. 1 O.R. sick to hospital. 1 O.R. returns to duty. | Nil. |
| | 5/1/17 | | 2.O.R. proceeded on leave. | S.I. |
| | | | 1.O.R. returns to duty from leave. | |
| | 6/1/17 | | 1 O R proceeded on leave. | N S.I. |
| | | | 1 O R admitted hospital | |
| | | | 1 O R attached sanitary section for instruction | |
| | 7/1/17. | | 1 O R proceeded on leave | S.I. |
| | 8/1/17 | | 1 O R proceeded on leave | |
| | | | 1 Officer Lt L.C. HALL. & 2 O R return to duty from leave or | |
| | | | 1 O R returns to duty from sanitary section. | |
| | | | 1 O R admitted hosp sick | |
| | | | 1 O R returns from hospital. | |

# WAR DIARY
## INTELLIGENCE SUMMARY

Army Form C. 2118

| Place | Date | Hour | Summary of Events and Information | Remarks and references to Appendices |
|---|---|---|---|---|
| PICQUIGNY. | 9/1/17 | | 2.O.R. proceeded on leave. | W.S.P. |
| | | | 10 R. return to duty from hospital | W.S.P. |
| DAOURS | 10/1/17 | | Dismounted section of Co. moved to DAOURS. | W.S.P. |
| | | | Transport moved from PICQUIGNY to CORBIE | |
| | | | 10 R. proceeded on leave | W.S.P. |
| | 11/1/17 | | 10 R. proceeded on leave | W.S.P. |
| | | | 10 R. admitted hospital sick | W.S.P. |
| | | | 1 Officer return to duty (Capt T R J MORGAN) (from Le PARCQ) | W.S.P. |
| | | | 1 O R. return to duty (batman) | W.S.P. |
| | 12/1/17 | | 2 O R. proceeded on leave | |
| | 13/1/17 | | 1 Officer (Lt W.H. NEVELL) & 2 O.R. (advance party) proceed by Rail to forward area to take over | O.S.P./R |
| | | | from 77 Fld. Co. R.E. | |
| | 14/1/17 | | 10 R. proceeds on leave. | O.S.P./R |
| | | | 10 R. joins Divl. SCHOOL | |
| | | | 10 R. at Divl. SCHOOL to take charge of pontoons re. | |
| | | | MAJOR A.F.G. RUSTON return to duty from leave. | |
| | 15/1/17 | | 2 O R. proceed on leave. | O.S.P./R |
| | | | 1 O R. (MEAULTE party) admitted hosp. (sick) | |
| | | | Co. move to MEAULTE | |
| NEAULTE | 16/1/17 | | 10 R. admitted H.o.sp. (sick) | O.S.P./R |
| | | | 1 Officer + 3 O.R. return to duty from leave. | |

# WAR DIARY
## INTELLIGENCE SUMMARY
*(Erase heading not required.)*

Army Form C. 2118

| Place | Date 1917 | Hour | Summary of Events and Information | Remarks and references to Appendices |
|---|---|---|---|---|
| MEAULTE | 16/1 | | Company proceeds to S29 c.3.2. Bivouacy at MEAULTE. 1/Lt. T. BUCKLEY, 220 O.R. (2 dismd.) to 7O.R. (N.H.) | O.5/R |
| | 15/1 | | 1/Lt. W.H. NEVELL takes out duties of D.O.R.E. B.&K AREAS, 3 O.R. att'd to D.O.R.E. for works | O.5/R |
| | 17/1 | | 1 O.R. att'd batm. for mnth. @ PLATEAU RAILHEAD<br>Lt. L.C. HALL relieves 1/Lt. T. BUCKLEY as O.B. Detachment @ MEAULTE.<br>Lt. T. BUCKLEY relieves 1/Lt. W.H. NEVELL as D.O.R.E. 1/Lt. NEVELL rejoins Co.<br>1 O.R. joins D.O.R.E. (batman)<br>2 O.R. return to duty from leave. | |
| | 18/1 | | 1 O.R. sick to Hospital. 1 O.R. returns to duty from leave (MEAULTE Det.) | O.5/R |
| | 19/1 | | 5 O.R. att'd D.O.R.E. | O.5/R |
| | 20/1 | | — | O.5/R |
| | 21/1 | | Capt. P.R.J. MORGAN proceeds on short leave to ABBEVILLE.<br>8 O.R. attached D.O.R.E. | O.5/R |
| | 22/1 | | 5 O.R. return to duty from leave.<br>1 O.R. admitted hosp. (sick) | O.5/R |
| | 23/1 | | 2 O.R. (N.H.) join Meaulte Detachment<br>Capt. P.R.J. MORGAN returns from leave. | O.5/R |
| | 24/1 | | 3 O.R. return from leave. | O.5/R |
| | 25/1 | | — | O.5/R |
| | 26/1 | | 2 O.R. admitted Hosp. (MEAULTE Det). 1 O.R. transferred from Dm. to M. service. | O.5/R |

# WAR DIARY
## INTELLIGENCE SUMMARY

Army Form C. 2118

| Place | Date | Hour | Summary of Events and Information | Remarks and references to Appendices |
|---|---|---|---|---|
| S27C32 BERNAFAY WOOD | 27/1/17 | | 20R. ret'd to duty from leave | BEF |
| | 28/1 | | 1OR. " " " " Blue Depot | OEF |
| | 29/1 | | 1 " " " " | OEF |
| | 30/1 | | 2UR. att. 10.M. XIV corps. | W. |
| | 31/1 | | Major R. att. Rota Pet'l to Le PARCQ. | W. |
| | | | Mons. EYMARD known as man. | |
| | | | 11 Lt. CAN. Kitchen. offices in town Major Ville. | |

31/1/17

Capt. R&CT
o/c 1/3 Kent F.A. G. OE.

Confidential./

Vol XI

War Diary.

497th (Kent) Field Co., R.E.

February 1st to February 28th 1917.

Volume XVII

Confidential./

# WAR DIARY or INTELLIGENCE SUMMARY

Army Form C. 2118

| Place | Date | Hour | Summary of Events and Information | Remarks and references to Appendices |
|---|---|---|---|---|
| BERNAFAY WOOD | 1/2/17 | — | Interior men on leave to S. France. | W. |
| " | 2/2/17 | | M/t men proceed to England (Cadt. ACR/7350. dat. 29/1/17 | W. |
| " | 3/2/17 | | | W. |
| " | 4/2/17 | | | W. |
| " | 5/2/17 | | | W. |
| " | 6/2/17 | | 10.R. to Hospital. 1 Offr. n/s Bentley & 140.R. 2/6th man unit from D.H.Q. 2.O.R. return from 10.M. XIV Corps. | |
| H n | 7/2/17 | | Corp. men to Helly At Hau & 3.O.R. m/t unit at Meaulte. 2/9 return from leave. 5.O.R. to hospital. 10.R. m/t Boys leave U.K. | W. |
| Heilly | 8/2/17 | | 1.O.R. (2nd Cpt Adamson) proceeds to England. | W. |

# WAR DIARY
or
INTELLIGENCE SUMMARY

*(Erase heading not required.)*

Army Form C. 2118

| Place | Date | Hour | Summary of Events and Information | Remarks and references to Appendices |
|---|---|---|---|---|
| Kelly | 9/2/17 | 10 R | — Leave to U.K. | WS |
| | | 60 R | to Hospital. | WS |
| | 10/2/17 | 10 R | to Hospital. | WS |
| | | 10 R | (Sent Fwd) returns from (Army School) | WS |
| | | 20 R | to Hospital | WS |
| | 11/2/17 | 40 R | return to duty from Hospital | |
| | 12/2/17 | 40 R | to Hospital | |
| | | 20 R | attached 10M. Fld Cav? | WS |
| | | 10 R | to Hospital 31.1.17 in England | |
| | | | —lights return from leave & returns to | |
| | | | Fort Review same day. | WS |
| | 13/2/17 | 20 R | return to duty from Hospital | WS |
| | | 10 R | return to duty from 29. Fld School | WS |
| | | | a) Instructor Gordon. Coy. for duty. | |
| | 14/2/17 | 10 R | to Hospital. joins | WS |
| | | M. LORENZ | | |

# WAR DIARY or INTELLIGENCE SUMMARY

Army Form C. 2118

| Place | Date | Hour | Summary of Events and Information | Remarks and references to Appendices |
|---|---|---|---|---|
| HEILLY | 15/2/17 | | | |
| | 16/2/17 | | 2 O.R. to Hospital. 2 O.R. return to duty from 1.O.M. Fld. Cdy. | |
| | 17/2/17 | | | |
| | 18/2/17 | | Major A.F.G. RUSTON returns to duty from Hospital. 1 Rotman return to duty. Lt. L.C. HALL & Lt. F.G. HUGGINS & 30 O.R. go to forward area to advance party. | ADS/R ADS/R |
| | 19/2/17 | | 3 O.R. admitted Hospital. 1 O.R. returned to duty. 1 O.R. proceed to Base (under age) | |
| | 20/2/17 | | Company move to MANSEL CAMP | |
| MANSEL CAMP | 21/2/17 | | 4 O.R. (reinforcements) join unit. Remainder of Company less 3 batmen, Mounted Section, Section 2 & 4 H.Q. Section attached proceed to COMBLES (H.Q.3 @ ATTACHMENTS) Excepted details proceed to WEDGEWOOD CAMP | ADS/R ADS/R |
| COMBLES | | | | |

# WAR DIARY
## or
## INTELLIGENCE SUMMARY

*(Erase heading not required.)*

Army Form C. 2118

| Place | Date 1917 | Hour | Summary of Events and Information | Remarks and references to Appendices |
|---|---|---|---|---|
| COMBLES | 22/2/17 | | 1 O.R. returns to duty from Hospital | O97/R |
| | 23/2 | | 1 Hants Reg. & Essex Regt attached to 5 S.R. London R.E. att for rations | O97/R |
| | 24/2 | | 1 O.R. Hants. Reg. att for duty & rations | |
| | | | 1 Dr. A.C. Boyce returns to duty from leave. Regarding ordnance manufacturing recently proceed to Base P.B. | |
| | 25/2 | | 1 O.R. (HANTS)(att for rations) admitted Hospital | O97/R |
| | | | 1 O.R. returns from Hospital to duty | |
| | 26/2 | | 1 O.R. (ESSEX)(att for rations) admitted Hospital | O97/R |
| | | | 3 O.R. admitted Hospital (sick) | |
| | | | 1 O.R. returns to duty from Hosp. | |
| | 27/2 | | 1 O.R. proceeds on leave to U.K. | O97/R |
| | | | 1 O.R. returns to duty from Hospital | |
| | | | 1 O.R. admitted Hospital | |
| | | | 2 O.R. proceed Ponton Park Devours | O97/R |
| | 28/2 | | 1 O.R. returned to duty from Hospital | O97/R |

O97/Ruston
Major R.E.(T)
O.C. 497 (Kent) Fld. Co. R.E.

CONFIDENTIAL.

WAR DIARY

OF

497th (Kent) Field Co., R.E.

From 1st March, 1917 To 31st March, 1917.

(VOLUME XVIII)

Army Form C. 2118

# WAR DIARY
## or
## INTELLIGENCE SUMMARY
(Erase heading not required.)

Instructions regarding War Diaries and Intelligence Summaries are contained in F. S. Regs., Part II. and the Staff Manual respectively. Title Pages will be prepared in manuscript.

| Place | Date 1917 | Hour | Summary of Events and Information | Remarks and references to Appendices |
|---|---|---|---|---|
| COMBLES | 1/3 | — | — | |
| | 2/3 | | 6.O.R. admitted Hosp. (Swounded & Passed) | OO4/R |
| | | | 2.O.R. return to Duty from 232 A.T.Co. (LOOP SIDING) | |
| | | | 10.R. return to Duty from XIV Corps Siding TRONES WOOD | |
| | | | 10.R. (A/Sgt. BOYCE) & Bo.R. proceed to HEILLY as advance party | |
| | 3/3 | | R/Sgt. P.J. MORGAN admitted Hospital | OO4/R |
| | | | Bo. proceeds to MÉAULTE (Boo) (L.E.G. HUGGINS) | |
| | 4/3 | | 1 man returns to duty from Hospital | OO4/R |
| | | | Bo. proceed to HEILLY. | |
| | 5/3 | | 10.R. admitted Hospital | OO4/R |
| | 6/3 | | CSM. HARDING, J. Transferred to establishment for Engineer Services | O5/R |
| | 7/3 | | A/Sgt. BOYCE admitted Hospital | O5/R |
| | | | 2.O.R. returns to duty from (D.M. XIV Corps | O5/R |
| | 8/3 | | — | |
| | 9/3 | | 10.R. returns to duty from Hospital | OO4/R |
| | | | 10.R. " " " " " DAOURS | |
| | 10/3 | | R/Sgt. MORGAN returns to duty from Hospital | OO4/R |
| | | | 2.O.R. return to duty from DAOURS | |
| | | | 10.R. (M.S.) return to duty from Leave | |
| | | | 2.O.R. proceed to Duty Gyroscope School | |

# WAR DIARY
## or
## INTELLIGENCE SUMMARY

*(Erase heading not required.)*

Army Form C. 2118

| Place | Date 1917 | Hour | Summary of Events and Information | Remarks and references to Appendices |
|---|---|---|---|---|
| NEILLY | 11/3 | | P.D.R. admitted Hospital | 002/R |
| | 12/3 | | 10.R. admitted Hospital | 003/R |
| | | | 6.O.R. admitted camp | |
| | 13/3 | | 10.R. returned to duty from hospital | 004/R |
| | | | 10.R. Transferred to 3rd Aus. Gen. R.C. | |
| | | | Lecture on Tuberculosis by R.M.O. | |
| | 14/3 | | 10.R. Hospital from U.K. | |
| | 15/3 | | 10.R. to School of Instruction | |
| | | | 2.O.R. admitted Hospital | 005/R |
| | 16/3 | | 10.R. admitted Hospital | 006/R |
| | | | 10.R. returned to duty from Hospital | |
| | 17/3 | | 10.R. proceeds on leave U.K. | 007/R |
| | 18/3 | | 30.R. admitted Hospital | 008/R |
| | | | Advance Party : Lt. HALL & 10.O.R. proceed to SAISSEVAL | |
| | 19/3 | | 10.R. admitted Hospital | 009/R |
| | | | 20.R. Transferred to Base (P.B.) | |
| | | | Transport marches to DADEURS | |
| SAISSEVAL | 20/3 | | Go proceeds to SAISSEVAL : 1 Off. & 25 O.R. on cycles by road, remnt. by Tactical Transport from EDGEHILL to AIRAINES. | 010/R |
| | | | Transport moves to ARGOEUVES | |

# WAR DIARY
or
## INTELLIGENCE SUMMARY
*(Erase heading not required.)*

Army Form C. 2118

| Place | Date 1917 | Hour | Summary of Events and Information | Remarks and references to Appendices |
|---|---|---|---|---|
| SAISSEVAL | 21/3 | | 10.O.R. admitted Hospital. | |
| | 22/3 | | 2.O.R. rett to duty from Divisional General School | OO7/R |
| | | | Transport arrived SAISSEVEL | OO7/R |
| | | | 2.O.R. admitted Hospital. | OO7/R |
| | 23/3 | | 3.O.R. " " | OO7/R |
| | | | 15 O.R. temporary draft from Co. | |
| | | | 3.O.R. Transferred to estab. of CRE 29th D von. | OO7/R |
| | 24/3 | | 2.O.R. return to duty from Hospital. | |
| | 25/3 | | 1.O.R. admitted Hospital | OO7/R |
| | | | 1.O.R. rett to duty from Hospital. | |
| | 26/3 | | 1.O.R. temporary draft from Co. | OO7/R |
| | | | 1.O.R. admitted Hospital | OO7/R |
| | | | 2.O.R. rett to duty from Hospital | OO7/R |
| | 27/3 | | 1.O.R. admitted Hosp. | |
| | | | 1.O.R. transferred to Base unfit. | |
| | 28/3 | | 1.O.R. returns to duty from School. | |
| | | | 2.O.R. admitted Hospital sick. | OO7/R |
| | | | 1.O.R. Transferred to I.W.T. Depot | |
| | 29/3 | | 2.O.R. admitted Hospital (sick) | OO7/R |

# WAR DIARY

## INTELLIGENCE SUMMARY

Army Form C. 2118

| Place | Date | Hour | Summary of Events and Information | Remarks and references to Appendices |
|---|---|---|---|---|
| SAISSEVAL | 30/3 1917 | | Company moves by Road to PERNOISE via PICQUIGNY & VIGNACOURT. | O.C.4R |
| PERNOISE | 31/3 | | 10.R. 4/mo Company from Reserve | O.C.4R |
| | | | 10.R. attached 29th Dn. W.R. (G.S.) | |

O.C.R Master
Major R.E.17
O.E. 4th W.R. Dn. 69. R.E.

CONFIDENTIAL

War Diary

of

497th (Kent) Field Co., R.E.

From 1st April, 1917       To 30th April, 1917

VOLUME XIX.

# WAR DIARY or INTELLIGENCE SUMMARY

Army Form C. 2118

(Erase heading not required.)

| Place | Date | Hour | Summary of Events and Information | Remarks and references to Appendices |
|---|---|---|---|---|
| PERNOISE | 1/4 1917 | | Company move north 86th Inf. Bde. via FIEFFES & CANDAS to | |
| GEZAIN-COURT | 2/4 | | GEZAINCOURT. 10.R. joins Company from Leave. Strength: 6 officers, 54 O/R., 1 Motorcycle + 135 P.M. + 48 Mules Tet. O.Ranks. Company arrives with 86th Inf. Bde. (by road) via DOULLENS to | O3/R |
| POMMERA | 3/4 | | POMMERA. 10.R. to Hospital (sick) | O3/R |
| | 4/4 | | 10.R. returns to duty from Hospital. 10.R. att'd 5 N.5 R.E.Park. | O3/R |
| | 5/4 | | 10.R. Transferred to Indraputation Troops BOULOGNE | O3/R |
| | | | Co. moves with 86th Inf. Bde. (by road) via LUCHEUX, SUS ST. LEGER + BAUDRICOURT to | |
| OPPY | 6/4 | | OPPY | O3/R |
| WARLUZEL | 7/4 | | 3.O.R. sick to Hospital. Company moves to WARLUZEL. | O3/R |
| HUMBER-CAMPS | 8/4 | | Company moves to HUMBERCAMPS | O3/R |
| | 9/4 | | 2.O.R. sick to Hospital. | O3/R |
| | 9/4 | | 3.O.R. rejoin Company from C.C.S. | O3/R |
| | 10/4 | | 10.R. returns from Leave. | O3/R |

**Army Form C. 2118.**

# WAR DIARY
## or
## INTELLIGENCE SUMMARY.
*(Erase heading not required.)*

Instructions regarding War Diaries and Intelligence Summaries are contained in F.S. Regs., Part II. and the Staff Manual respectively. Title pages will be prepared in manuscript.

| Place | Date | Hour | Summary of Events and Information | Remarks and references to Appendices |
|---|---|---|---|---|
| Humincourt | 10/4/17 | — | Coy. Comm. Humincourt + proc to Simencourt. | JW. |
| | 10/5/17 | | 20.R. to Hospital. | JW. |
| | 11/5/17 | | 10.R. left @ HUMBER CAMP in charge of Coy. Transp. | |
| Simencourt | 11/5/17 | | 10.R. to Hospital. | JW. |
| | | | 10.R. returns to duty from Hospital. | |
| | | | 20.R. return to duty from Hospital. | |
| Simencourt | 12/5/17 | | Coy. Comm. SIMENCOURT + proc to ARRAS. | JW. |
| | | | 10.R. left in charge of Coy. Transp. | |
| | | | Coy. move to Trenches @ G.30.c.5.4. Transport remain @ ARRAS. | |
| ARRAS | 13/5/17 | | | JW. |
| | 14/5/14 | | Coy. move to Trenches @ N.3.A.6.7 Transport remains at ARRAS. | JW. |
| | 15/5/14 | | 10.R. to Hospital sick. | JW. |
| | | | 10.R. returns to duty from Hospital. | |
| | | | 10.R. Killed. (19968 Gr. JENNER). | |

Army Form C. 2118.

# WAR DIARY
## or
## INTELLIGENCE SUMMARY.
(Erase heading not required.)

Instructions regarding War Diaries and Intelligence Summaries are contained in F.S. Regs., Part II. and the Staff Manual respectively. Title pages will be prepared in manuscript.

| Place | Date | Hour | Summary of Events and Information | Remarks and references to Appendices |
|---|---|---|---|---|
| ARRAS | 16/4/17 | | 4 O.R. wounded. | W |
| | | | 10 O.R. wounded return to duty not diary. | SG |
| | 17/4/17 | | Forward section of Company move to TILLOY QUARRY H.32.c.05.65 | SG |
| | 18/4/17 | | 1 O.R. to Hospital wounded. night 16/17. | |
| | 19/4/17 | | 1 O.R. wounded. | |
| | 20/4/17 | | | |
| | 21/4/17 | | 1 O.R. to Hospital sick. | W |
| | 22/4/17 | | 2 O.R. return to duty from Hospital. | |
| | | | 6 O.R. draft join Coy. | |
| | 23/4/17 | | 1 O.R. - to duty from Hospital. | W |
| | | | a/t Neal London R.E. attached to Coy. for Duty | |
| | 24/4/17 | | 1 O.R. trans. to 1/B Field Survey Coy. R.E. Southampton. | |

Army Form C. 2118.

# WAR DIARY
## INTELLIGENCE SUMMARY.
*(Erase heading not required.)*

Instructions regarding War Diaries and Intelligence Summaries are contained in F. S. Regs. Part II. and the Staff Manual respectively. Title pages will be prepared in manuscript.

| Place | Date 1917 | Hour | Summary of Events and Information | Remarks and references to Appendices |
|---|---|---|---|---|
| ARRAS BERNEVILLE | 25/4 | | Company marches to BERNEVILLE into billets | AAR |
| WANQUETIN | 26/4 | | Company marches to WANQUETIN into billets | AAR |
| FONQUE-VILLERS | 27/4 | | Company marches to FONQUEVILLERS | AAR |
| | 28/4 | | 10.R. from Company but remains @ Corps Depot. 80.R. reinforcing draft from Bo. 10.R. admitted Hospital (sick) | AAR AAR AAR |
| | 29/4 | | 10.R. " " | |
| | 30/4 | | Effective Strength :- 5 Officers 1 Offr attached 1 W.O. hospital 135 O.R. Dismounted 50 O.R. Mounted. | |

A.P. Proton
Major R.E. (T.)
O.G. 497th (Kent) Field Co. R.E.

C O N F I D E N T I A L

War Diary

of

497TH (KENT) FIELD CO., R.E.

From 1st May, 1917 to 31st May, 1917

V O L U M E   XX

-o-o-o-o-

Army Form C. 2118.

# WAR DIARY
## or
## INTELLIGENCE SUMMARY.
*(Erase heading not required.)*

Instructions regarding War Diaries and Intelligence Summaries are contained in F. S. Regs., Part II. and the Staff Manual respectively. Title pages will be prepared in manuscript.

| Place | Date 1917 | Hour | Summary of Events and Information | Remarks and references to Appendices |
|---|---|---|---|---|
| FONQUE- VILLERS | 1/5 | | Company arrived by rail (with Bde.) to | OO71/R |
| GOUY-EN- ARTOIS | | | GOUY-EN-ARTOIS (in billets) | |
| do | 2/5 | | Company moved by road (with Bde.) to ARRAS | OO73/R |
| ARRAS | 3/5 | | Arrived ARRAS (in billets) | OO74/R |
| | 4/5 | | — | OO75/R |
| | 5/5 | | — | OO76/R |
| | 6/5 | | — | OO77/R |
| | 7/5 | | 2O.R. proceed to 29th Divisional Gas School, St Pôl for course of instruction. 1O.R. proceeded to No.8 R.E. Park to ?relieve Sappers in charge of Pontoon Equipment who returns to Company (Lieut. ROSS A. SMITH M.C., Lt. E.G. HUGGINS, & 57 O.R. (2 M.T.)) moved to | OO78/R |
| DAINVILLE | | | DAINVILLE by road (billets) | |
| | 8/5 | | 10.R. to Hospital (sick) | OO81/R |
| | | | 10.R. returns from C.R.E. | |
| | 9/5 | | 2O.R. admitted Hospital (sick) | OO82/R |
| | 10/5 | | Capt. P.R.J. MORGAN proceeds to 2.O.R. to return to INDIA OFFICE (A.G./G.H.Q./A./22707/18) | |
| | | | 10.R. admitted Hospital (sick) | |
| | | | 2O.R. return from 29 Divl Gas School | |
| | 11/5 | | 1O.R. admitted Hospital (sick) | OO84/R |
| | | | 15O.R. join Co as reinforcing draft. | OO85/R |

Army Form C. 2118.

# WAR DIARY
## INTELLIGENCE SUMMARY.
*(Erase heading not required.)*

Instructions regarding War Diaries and Intelligence Summaries are contained in F. S. Regs., Part II. and the Staff Manual respectively. Title pages will be prepared in manuscript.

| Place | Date 1917 | Hour | Summary of Events and Information | Remarks and references to Appendices |
|---|---|---|---|---|
| DAINVILLE | 10/5 | | 10.R. admitted Hospital (sick) ARRAS DET | OC/R |
| | 11/5 | | 2/Lt. GEA. DISTURNAL attached to Co. from H.S.E. (Aldershot) H.Q. Co. R.E. | OC/R |
| | | | 5/E.G. HUGGINS & 1 O.R. reinforcements rejoin Co. from H.S.E. @ DAINVILLE | OC/R |
| | 12/5 | | 11/H.S.A. SMITH attached to ARRAS DET by Mt. A.F. NEAL | OC/R |
| | | | 1 O.R. proceeds to XVIII Corps School for course of Instruction | OC/R |
| | 13/5 | | 1 O.R. to Hospital (sick) | OC/R |
| | 14/5 | | 3. O.R. reinforcing draft join Co. | |
| | | | 1 O.R. admitted Hospital (sick) | OC/R |
| | 15/5 | | Co. moves from DAINVILLE to ARRAS to H.32.a.8.2 & | OC/R |
| Infantry t ARRAS at H.32.a.8.2. | | | 15 O.R. detailed to work @ CRE dump (R.172) ARRAS. | OC/R |
| | 16/5 | | 7 O.R. joined Co. (Reinforcements) | |
| | | | 1 O.R. (N.A.) attd. 66th Bde. | |
| | | | 1 O.R. (85th Bde HQ) attd Co. 3 | |
| | 17/5 | | 10.R. joined Co. from No. 5. Reinforcement Co. R.E. | OC/R |
| | 18/5 | | 10.R. (Sgt) from Co. from anti-Depot to relieve 1 Sgt. from Co. | OC/R |
| | 19/5 | | 1 O.R. join Co. (reinforcement) | OC/R |
| | 20/5 | | 1 O.R. (Sgt) proceed to ahmi Depot. | OC/R |
| | | | 1 O.R. proceeds to U.K. on leave | |
| | | | 1 O.R. rejoins Co. from Hospital | |
| | | | M/Lt. G.E.A. DISTURNAL rejoins his Company. | OC/R |

Army Form C. 2118.

# WAR DIARY
# INTELLIGENCE SUMMARY.

(Erase heading not required.)

Instructions regarding War Diaries and Intelligence Summaries are contained in F. S. Regs., Part II. and the Staff Manual respectively. Title pages will be prepared in manuscript.

| Place | Date 1917 | Hour | Summary of Events and Information | Remarks and references to Appendices |
|---|---|---|---|---|
| #52a 92. | 21/5 | | 2/O.R. proceed to U.K. on leave | O.C.P.R |
| | | | 1/O.R. returns to duty from Hospital | O.C.P.R |
| | 22/5 | | #/Lt. E.R. HUGGINS and 2 other ranks wounded to Hosp. | |
| | | | 1/O.R. missing believed wounded. | |
| | | | 2/O.R. from #64 O.T. attached to Co for fit rations | |
| | 23/5 | | 2/O.R. admitted Hospital (sick) | |
| | | | 4/O.R. sent reinforcements from Bompong | |
| | | | 1/O.R. return to duty from Hospital | O.C.P.R |
| | | | 1/O.R. proceed to U.K. on leave | |
| | 24/5 | | 1/O.R. proceed to U.K. on leave | O.C.P.R |
| | | | 12/O.R. reinforcing draft join Company | |
| | | | 1/O.R. (Draft) previously shown as attached to Company, now posted | |
| | 25/5 | | 1/O.R. admitted Hospital (sick) | O.C.P.R |
| | | | 1/O.R. proceed on leave to U.K. | |
| | | | 1/O.R. rejoins Co from base Depot | |
| | 26/5 | | — | O.C.P.R. |
| | 27/5 | | 2/O.R. admitted Hospital | O.C.P.R |
| | | | 1/O.R. proceed on leave, U.K. | O.C.P.R |
| | 28/5 | | — | |

Army Form C. 2118.

# WAR DIARY
## or
## INTELLIGENCE SUMMARY.
*(Erase heading not required.)*

Instructions regarding War Diaries and Intelligence Summaries are contained in F. S. Regs., Part II. and the Staff Manual respectively. Title pages will be prepared in manuscript.

| Place | Date 1917 | Hour | Summary of Events and Information | Remarks and references to Appendices |
|---|---|---|---|---|
| H32 a 8.2. | 29/5 | | 16 R. admitted hospital. | |
| | | | 30 R. admitted Botho Rackstohn. | |
| | | | 10 R. returns to duty from hospital. | |
| | | | 10 R. previously reported "missing believed wounded" now reported "Missing believed Killed." | 009/R |
| | | 30/5 | 10 R. returns to duty from hospital | 009/R |
| | | | 10 R. Joins Bn. from SIMENCOURT. | 009/R |
| | | 31/5 | 10 R. proceeds on leave to U.K. fortnight. | |
| | | | Strength: 4 Officers (one on duty in U.K.) | |
| | | | 1 Officer att'd to 510th London Fld. Co. R.E. | |
| | | | 1 Interpreter | |
| | | | 175 O.R. dismounted | |
| | | | 58 O.R. Mounted. | |

O.J.Ruston
Major R.T.T.
O.C. 497th (Kent) Fld. Co. R.E.

CONFIDENTIAL.

War Diary

of

497th (Kent) Field Co., R.E.

From 1st June, 1917   To 30th June, 1917.

VOLUME   XXI.

# WAR DIARY

## INTELLIGENCE SUMMARY.

*(Erase heading not required.)*

Army Form C. 2118.

Instructions regarding War Diaries and Intelligence Summaries are contained in F.S. Regs., Part II. and the Staff Manual respectively. Title pages will be prepared in manuscript.

| Place | Date 1917 | Hour | Summary of Events and Information | Remarks and references to Appendices |
|---|---|---|---|---|
| M TILLOY } H52 A8.2. } | 1/6 | — | 1.O.R. (Blair & 3) joins Co. as return guide. Major A.F.G. RUSTON takes up duties of A/CRE during absence on leave of Lt. Col. BIDDULPH. 1.O.R. wounded accidentally (bomb) | 057/R |
|  | 2/6 | — | Company moves from H.82 A.8.2. & Transport from Enemy Zone FAUBOURG RONVILLE to BERNEVILLE. 1.O.R. joins unit from A.S.C. 1.O.R. (attached) joins A.S.C. on return journey. | 057/R |
| BERNEVILLE |  |  |  |  |
|  | 3/6 |  | T/Lt NEAL & Interpreter LORENZ proceed in advance to GORGES. Company (less transport & cyclists) arrvd. St. L.C. HALL + 112 O.R. proceed by road to BEAUMETZ – RIVIERE & thence by tactical train to FIENVILLERS – CANDAS, & thence by road to GORGES. Transport proceeded by road to LUCHEUX via MONDICOURT (contd. on 6th) | 057/R |
| GORGES |  |  | 1.O.R. rejoins unit from No.5 REPARK. | 057/R |
|  | 4/6 |  | Transport cyclists march by road to GORGES. | 057/R |
|  | 5/6 |  | 1.O.R. returns to duty from MAXIMUM CAMP. | 057/R |
|  | 7/6 |  | 2.O.R. return to duty from leave. | 057/R |
|  |  |  | 11 Lts. W.E. DARLINGTON, W.H. LUDLOW + A.G. TOOMEY (attached) join Company as reinforcements. |  |
|  |  |  | 1.O.R. returns to duty from hospital. |  |
|  |  |  | 15 O.R. join Co. as reinforcing draft. |  |
|  | 6/6 |  | 1.O.R. rejoins Co. from leave. | 057/R |
|  | 8/6 |  | 2.O.R. rejoin Co. from leave. 1.O.R. rejoins Co. from SG.9 Inf. Bde. H.Q. | 057/R |
|  |  |  | 3.O.R. (reinforcing draft) from Base. | 057/R |

**Army Form C. 2118.**

# WAR DIARY
## INTELLIGENCE SUMMARY.
*(Erase heading not required.)*

Instructions regarding War Diaries and Intelligence Summaries are contained in F. S. Regs., Part II. and the Staff Manual respectively. Title pages will be prepared in manuscript.

| Place | Date | Hour | Summary of Events and Information | Remarks and references to Appendices |
|---|---|---|---|---|
| GORGES | 1917 | | | |
| | 9/6 | | 2 O.R. admitted Hospital (sick) | O.S.R. |
| | 10/6 | | 1 O.R. rejoined Co. from leave | O.S.R. |
| | 11/6 | | 1 O.R. to Hqrs Co. for School | O.S.R. |
| | | | 10 O.R. joined Co. (Reinforcement) | |
| | 12/6 | | 1 O.R. admitted Hosp (sick) | O.S.R. |
| | | | 1 O.R. rejoined Co. from Hosp. | |
| | | | 1 O.R. rejoined Co. from Leave. | |
| | 13/6 | | 1/Lt A.F. NEAL proceeded on leave to U.K. | O.S.R. |
| | 14/6 | | 1 O.R. admitted Hosp. (sick) | O.S.R. |
| | | | 1 O.R. returned to duty from Hosp. | O.S.R. |
| | 15/6 | | 1 O.R. admitted Hosp. (sick) | O.S.R. |
| | 16/6 | | 16 Officers (14 SOMERS) + 78 O.R. attached to Co. for discipline rations for instruction in dug out work. | O.S.R. |
| | 17/6 | | 1/Lt S.A. SMITH proceeded on leave to U.K. | O.S.R. |
| | | | 2 O.R. admitted Hosp (sick). 1 O.R. rejoined Co. from Hospital. | |
| | 18/6 | | 1 O.R. admitted Hosp. (sick) | O.S.R. |
| | | | 1 O.R. (attached) admitted Hosp. (sick) | O.S.R. |
| | 19/6 | | 1 O.R. (Infantry) admitted Hospital | O.S.R. |
| | | | 1/Lt C.D. RIDDEL joins company as reinforcement. 10 O.R. attached Company for rations. | O.S.R. |

# WAR DIARY
## INTELLIGENCE SUMMARY
*(Erase heading not required.)*

Army Form C. 2118.

Instructions regarding War Diaries and Intelligence Summaries are contained in F.S. Regs. Part II. and the Staff Manual respectively. Title pages will be prepared in manuscript.

| Place | Date 1917 | Hour | Summary of Events and Information | Remarks and references to Appendices |
|---|---|---|---|---|
| GORGES | 20/6 | | 10.R. admitted Hospital. | O.O./R |
| | 21/6 | | 10.R. returns to duty from Hospital. 10.R. rejoins Co. from Brigade School. 20.R. admitted Hospital. 10.R. (Infantry & Bryant party) admitted Hospital. 9.O.R. attached for Rations " 10.R. proceeds on leave to U.K. | |
| | 22/6 | | 1 Officer & 75 Infantry attached for transport in dug out work return to Unit Ventb. | O.O./R |
| | 23/6 | | 10.R. proceeds to U.K. on leave. | O.O./R |
| | 24/6 | | 20.R. attached to Co. for return. Flt. C.D. RIDDEL & 1 O.R. (attached) leave Co. & join 510 (London) Field Co. R.E. 1.O.R. proceeds in advance to POPERINGHE. | O.O./R O.O./R |
| | 25/6 | | 10.R. proceeds on leave 10.R. (transferred to R.O.P.) leaves Co. | |
| | 26/6 | | Company moves by road to CANDAS-FIENVILLERS thence by train to REXPOEDE 10/R. (Lt. L.C. HALL) proceeds on leave to U.K. | |
| PROVEN. | 27/6 | 10 a.m. | Company arrives at REXPOEDE and marches to PROVEN | |

# WAR DIARY
## INTELLIGENCE SUMMARY

Army Form C. 2118.

(Erase heading not required.)

| Place | Date | Hour | Summary of Events and Information | Remarks and references to Appendices |
|---|---|---|---|---|
| PROVEN | 27/6 | | 174 AT NEAL rejoins Hors from Leave. 1 O.R. (attached) rejoins unit. Lt. TOOLEY on 6 h. Meadlam observed. WEST CANAL BANK MARENGO HOUSE. | CopyR |
| C19 c 1.6. | 28/6 | | 6 O.R. (attached) rejoin units. Company (less Stores below) proceeds by quarters at C19 c 1.6. relieving 157 F.O. Co. R.E. 22 O.R. proceed to Dul. Workshops. 11/Lt DARLINGTON + 16 O.R. (Mounted) + 120 O.R. (Dismounted) proceed to zone at VOXVUE FARM A15 d 37. | CopyR CopyR |
| | 29/6 | | 5 O.R. (attached) rejoin unit. 1 O.R. attached (R.E. M.LORENZ (Interpreter) proceeds on leave to U.K. M.J. MARINISSEN (Interpreter) joins Company | CopyR |
| | 30/6 | | Strength of Company. 7 Officers (1 Gumps on duty; 1 att'd) 2 Officers att'd 1 Interpreter 184 O.R. Dismounted 53 O.R. Mounted. | |

CoyRoirson
Major R.E.(T)
O.C. 497 "(Kent) Fd. Co. R.E.

CONFIDENTIAL.

War Diary

of

497th (Kent) Field Company R.E.

From 1st July, 1917 to 30th July, 1917.

VOLUME XXII.

**Army Form C. 2118.**

# WAR DIARY
## INTELLIGENCE SUMMARY.
*(Erase heading not required.)*

Instructions regarding War Diaries and Intelligence Summaries are contained in F. S. Regs., Part II. and the Staff Manual respectively. Title pages will be prepared in manuscript.

| Place | Date 1917 | Hour | Summary of Events and Information | Remarks and references to Appendices |
|---|---|---|---|---|
| C.19.c.1.6. | 1/7 | | Strength of Company: 7 Offrs. (one away on duty, one attd ~~attd~~ ) | |
| | | | 2 Offrs. attd | |
| | | | 1 Interpreter | |
| | | | 184 O.R. Drummed | |
| | | | 53 O.R. Mounted | |
| | | | 16.R. to Hospital (Wounded H.E. fuse) | O.O.P. |
| | | | 16.R. wounded at Duty. 1/Lt. S.A. SMITH returns to duty from leave. | |
| | 2/7 | | 1 O.R. wounded at Duty. | |
| | | | 1 O.R. proceeds on leave to U.K. | O.O.P. |
| | | | 1 O.R. returns from leave from Hospital. | O.O.P. |
| | 3/7 | | 1 O.R. wounded at duty | |
| | 4/7 | | 1 O.R. wounded at duty | |
| | | | 1 O.R. killed (H.E. shell) | O.O.P. |
| | | | 1 O.R. wounded to Hospital | O.O.P. |
| | 5/7 | | 1 O.R. proceeds on leave to U.K. | O.O.P. |
| | | | 2 O.R. return to duty from leave. | O.O.P. |
| | 6/7 | | — | |
| | 7/7 | | 1 O.R. returns to duty from leave. | O.O.P. |
| | 8/7 | | 2 O.R. admitted Hospital Sick | O.O.P. |

# WAR DIARY
## or
## INTELLIGENCE SUMMARY.
*(Erase heading not required.)*

Army Form C. 2118.

Instructions regarding War Diaries and Intelligence Summaries are contained in F. S. Regs., Part II. and the Staff Manual respectively. Title pages will be prepared in manuscript.

| Place | Date | Hour | Summary of Events and Information | Remarks and references to Appendices |
|---|---|---|---|---|
| Shuts 28 C.19.C.1.6. | 9/7 | | Lt. L.C. HALL returns to duty from leave. | |
| | | | 10 R. returns to duty from leave | 057/R |
| | | | 19 R. killed on duty | |
| | 10/7 | | 10 R. proceeds on leave to U.K. | |
| | | | 10 R. killed | |
| | | | 20 R. wounded | |
| | | | 10 R. returns to duty from hospital | 057/R |
| | | | 10 R. proceeds on leave | |
| | 11/7 | | Lt. L.C. HALL wounded (slight) | |
| | | | 30 R. wounded | |
| | 12/7 | | 10 R. proceeds on leave. M. MARINISSEN leaves Company. | 057/R |
| | 13/7 | | 10 R. wounded | 057/R |
| | | | 10 R. proceeds on leave | 057/R |
| | 14/7 | | — | |
| | 15/7 | | 10 R. returns to duty from leave. | 057/R |
| | | | 20 R. wounded | |
| | 16/7 | | 10 R. proceeds on leave | 057/R |
| | | | M. LORENZ returns to duty from leave | |

**Army Form C. 2118.**

# WAR DIARY
## —of—
## INTELLIGENCE SUMMARY.
*(Erase heading not required.)*

Instructions regarding War Diaries and Intelligence Summaries are contained in F. S. Regs., Part II. and the Staff Manual respectively. Title pages will be prepared in manuscript.

| Place | Date | Hour | Summary of Events and Information | Remarks and references to Appendices |
|---|---|---|---|---|
| Shot 20 C19 C1.6. | 17/7 | | 2.0.t. wounded | O.C./R |
| | 18/7 | | 2.0.t. wounded at duty. | |
| | | | 10.t. Admitted Hospital sick | O.C./R |
| | 19/7 | | 10R. Returns to duty from leave. | |
| | | | 20R. wounded. | |
| | | | 10R. wounded at duty. R.H.E.S. DAWES joins Company from base as Reinforcement | O.C./R |
| | 20/7 | | 10R. proceeds on leave. 16th | |
| | | | Company & Transport move to PROVEN N°3 AREA | |
| | | | (19 S.E. / × 25 a 94.) | |
| | | | 1Lt TORKEY or 2.O.t. leaves for Fifth Army Rest Camp | O.C./R |
| PROVEN | 21/7 | | 10R. returns to duty from leave. | O.C./R |
| | 22/7 | | — | O.C./R |
| | 23/7 | | 10R. proceeds on leave to U.K. | O.C./R |
| | 24/7 | | 20R. returns to duty from Leave. | |
| | | | 10R. returns to duty from C.R.E. | |
| | | | 10R. rejoins from hosp. | |
| | | | 10R. rejoins Brown Hospital. | |

**Army Form C. 2118.**

# WAR DIARY
## of
## INTELLIGENCE SUMMARY.
*(Erase heading not required.)*

Instructions regarding War Diaries and Intelligence Summaries are contained in F. S. Regs., Part II. and the Staff Manual respectively. Title pages will be prepared in manuscript.

| Place | Date 1917 | Hour | Summary of Events and Information | Remarks and references to Appendices |
|---|---|---|---|---|
| Rouen | 24/7/17 | | Lt. D. COMINS ♯10.R. arrived at Corps Depot from Base and taken on strength | 037/R |
| | 25/7/17 | | 10R. returns to duty from Hospital. Lt. W.H. CHAPMAN joins Company from V.R. (transferment) | 037/R |
| | | | 3 Officers + 105 O.R. attached 2. Co from 86th Inf Bde as Carrying Party | 037/R |
| | 26/7/17 | | 10R admitted Hospital (sick). 4 O.R. at 1 N.O. + 6 O.R. for work. | 037/R |
| | 27/7/17 | | 10R. wounded at duty 19/7/17 admitted Hospital from 2/8th Army Resn station | |
| | | | Lt. L.F.S. DAWES ♯10.R. admitted Hospital (sick) | 037/R |
| | 28/7/17 | | 10R. returns to duty from leave | |
| | | | 16R. rejoins Co. from Corps Depot | 037/R |
| | | | Lt. D. COMINS joins 29th Divl Engrs. + is attached to 510th (London) H.Q. 6. R.E. | 037/R |
| | 28/7/17 | | 10R. rejoins Co. from leave | |
| | 29/7/17 | | 10R. proc on leave to U.K. (10 days)   4 10.R. rejoin from NorR. R.E.I. (Works) | 037/R |
| | | | 10R. admitted hospital (sick) | |
| | | | Lt. L.C. HALL rejoins Co. from Base | |
| | 30/7/17 | | 1 OR. proc on leave to U.K (10 days) | |
| | | | 2 OR. admitted Hosp (sick) | |

Army Form C. 2118.

# WAR DIARY
## —or—
## INTELLIGENCE SUMMARY.
*(Erase heading not required.)*

| Place | Date | Hour | Summary of Events and Information | Remarks and references to Appendices |
|---|---|---|---|---|
| PROVEN | 30/7 1917 | | 1 O.R. (attached Infantry) admitted Hospital (sick) | O/C 4/R |
| | 31/7 | | 1 O.R. joins from Base | |
| | | | Strength of Company: 8 Officers (one of that attached to another Company) 1 attached Officer R.E. 1 Interpreter 170 O.R. dismounted 51 O.R. mounted | |
| | | | Infantry attached: 3 Officers } Carrying Party 104 O.R. } 1 Ration Guard 1 O.R. attached pending Transfer | O/C R. voln. Major R.E.(T) O.C. 497 (Kent) Fld. Co. R.E. |

CONFIDENTIAL.

War Diary

of

497th (Kent) Field Co.,R.E.

From 1st August, 1917. to 31st August, 1917.

VOLUME XXIII.

-*-*-

# WAR DIARY
## INTELLIGENCE SUMMARY.
*(Erase heading not required.)*

Army Form C. 2118.

| Place | Date | Hour | Summary of Events and Information | Remarks and references to Appendices |
|---|---|---|---|---|
| PROVEN | 1/8 | | 10.R. Returns Felsty from Hospital | O.O/R |
| | 2/8 | | 10.R attached to 18th M.V.S. for duty | O.O/R |
| | | | 1/Lt. A.G. TOOKEY & 1 1O.R. return to duty from 7/1/2 Army Rest Station | O.O/R |
| | 3/8 | | — | O.O/R |
| | 4/8 | | 10.R. proceeds on leave | |
| | | | Returns to duty from C.C.S. (Officer Servant) | |
| | 5/8 | | 10.R. (attached Infantry) Admitted Hospital (sick) | O.O/R |
| | | | 2.O.R. admitted Hospital (sick) | |
| | 6/8 | | 10.R. proceeds on leave | O.O/R |
| | | | 10.R. returns to duty from Hospital | |
| | | | 10.R. (Officers Servant) returns to C.C.S. 2.O.R. Base Co. to join 66th Wagon Erecting Co. R.E. | O.O/R |
| LUNAVILLE FARM | 7/8 | | Company (Mess Department + details) moved to LUNAVILLE FARM. Transport + details move to Camp in FOREST AREA. | |
| | | | 1.O.R. left at PROVEN as Camp Warden. | |
| | | | 1O.R. joins Co. from Base as Reinforcement | |
| | | | 10.R. proceeds on leave. | |
| | 8/8 | | 2.O.R. return to duty from Hospital | O.O/R |
| | | | 10.R. returns to duty from Hospital | O.O/R |
| | 9/8 | | 2O.R. (attached Infantry) returned | |
| | | | #/Lt. CRAWFORD (Royal Irish) Wounded at duty. | O.O/R |

# WAR DIARY
## —or—
## INTELLIGENCE SUMMARY.

(Erase heading not required.)

Army Form C. 2118.

| Place | Date 1917 | Hour | Summary of Events and Information | Remarks and references to Appendices |
|---|---|---|---|---|
| LUNAVILLE FARM | 10/8 | | 10.R. proceeds on leave. | O&R |
| | 11/8 | | 80.R. wounded | |
| | | | 10.R. (Officers Servant) returns to duty from C.C.S. | O&R |
| | 12/8 | | 10.R. [attached Infantry] wounded at Duty. | |
| | | | 10.R. proc on leave. | |
| | | | 10.R. returns to duty from leave. | |
| | 13/8 | | 10.R. goes on leave. | O&R |
| | | | 10.R. (attached Infantry) admitted Hosp. (sick) | O&R |
| | 14/8 | | 20.R. go on leave. | O&R |
| | | | 10.R. wounded. | |
| | | | 16.R. admitted Hosp. (sick) | |
| | | | 10.R. (attached) admitted Hosp. (sick) | |
| | | | 10.R. returned missing from 11/8/17 | |
| | 15/8 | | 10.R. proceeds on leave | O&R |
| | | | 20.R. returns to duty from Hospital. | O&R |
| | | | 20.R. returns to duty from leave | |
| | 16/8 | | 10.R. proceeds on leave, 70.R. wounded | |
| | | | 10.R. [attached infantry] wounded & succumbed of wounds | |
| | | In anticipation of operations on Europa Front, bombing material is being moved into F & redejions at BOIS FARM (28/3.6 & 6.3.) | |

A.5834  Wt. W4973/M687  750,000  8/16  D. D. & L. Ltd.  Forms/C.2118/13.

# WAR DIARY
## INTELLIGENCE SUMMARY
(Erase heading not required.)

Army Form C. 2118.

| Place | Date 1917 | Hour | Summary of Events and Information | Remarks and references to Appendices |
|---|---|---|---|---|
| LUNAVILLE FARM | 14/8 | Oct 8.15a.m | Notification received from Bde. that consolidation parties might now proceed forward in small parties. The following parties therefore proceeded forward with necessary stores:- <br> (i) No.1 party (2 Officers & 50 O.R. (R.E. & Infantry)) went to MARTIN MILL. They erected a Strong Point @ or near point 28/V22.c.1.3. The front in question must have been under observation for almost immediately after work was started the party was subjected to at first intermittent & then almost continuous shelling. The work was however completed with only 5 casualties (all returned, & one since died of wounds). It was noticed that an enemy aeroplane was flying backwards & forwards over this part of the line during the whole morning. Captured area at a height of little over 400 feet. Work was completed about 2 p.m. <br> (ii) No 2 party (of the same strength as No 1) went to DENAIN FARM. They moved to Strong Point @ or near point 28/V21.d.3.6. The party was practically undisturbed by enemy artillery & finished their work shortly after midday. <br> (iii) Joint parties (of combined strength of 3 Officers & 60 O.R. - R.E. & Infantry) worked on the bridges over the STEENBEEK from the YPRES-STADEN RAILWAY on the Right to the 38 Bde Boundary 100x to North of RUISSEAU FARM (28/V21.c.6.5.) on the Left. All the footbridges were finished but in order to stone main bridges were set in order & approaches made good. The last squad of these parties returned tat about 4 p.m. | |

# WAR DIARY
## INTELLIGENCE SUMMARY.
*(Erase heading not required.)*

Army Form C. 2118.

| Place | Date 1917 | Hour | Summary of Events and Information | Remarks and references to Appendices |
|---|---|---|---|---|
| LUNAVILLE FARM | 17/8 | | 1O.R. proceeds on leave. | A37/R |
| | 18/8 | | 1O.R. (attached Infantry) wounded at duty. 1O.R. (att Inf.) proc on leave. | A37/R A37/R |
| | | | 1OR proc on leave | |
| | | | 2OR wounded at duty. | |
| | 19/8 | | 1OR returns from leave. | |
| | 20/8 | | H.O.R. → proc on leave. | |
| | | | 1 OR. admitted Hospital (sick) | |
| | | | 1 OR. (att Inf.) admitted Hosp (sick) | |
| | | | " " (wounded) | |
| | | | 1 OR (att Inf) | |
| | 21/8 | | 8 OR proc on leave | A37/R |
| | | | 1 OR (att Inf.) wounded. | |
| | | | 3 OR return to duty from leave. | |
| | 22/8 | | 3 OR proc on leave. | A37/R |
| | | | 1 Lt. R.S. DAVIS and 1 OR. (Batman) attached to bn. | |
| | | | 1 OR. (Acq Sgt.) attached to Co. | |
| | 23/8 | | 1 Lt. A.G. TOOKEY from No.7 Pontoon Park, R.E. | A37/R |
| | | | 1 OR killed. | |
| | | | 1 OR wounded | |
| | | | H.O.R proc on leave. | A37/R |

**Army Form C. 2118.**

# WAR DIARY
## or
## INTELLIGENCE SUMMARY.
*(Erase heading not required.)*

Instructions regarding War Diaries and Intelligence Summaries are contained in F.S. Regs., Part II. and the Staff Manual respectively. Title pages will be prepared in manuscript.

| Place | Date | Hour | Summary of Events and Information | Remarks and references to Appendices |
|---|---|---|---|---|
| LUNAVILLE FARM | 1917 24/8 | | 4 O.R. farm leave (1 meantime attached C.R.E.) 10.R. attached C.R.E. | O4/R |
| | 26/8 | | 3 O.R. return from leave | O4/R |
| | 26/8 | | 3 O.R. proceeded to leave | |
| PORTSDOWN CAMP, PROVEN | | | Company & Transport moved from existing locations to PROVEN 3 AREA, PORTSDOWN CAMP. Sheet 19 X 25 a 7.3. | L.E.G. L.E.G. |
| | 27/8 | | 1 O.R. return from leave | |
| | 28/8 | | Major Paston proceeded on leave. 1 Reinforcement joined Coy. 2 O.R. proceeded L.E.G. on leave. 1 O.R. rejoined from leave. | L.E.G. |
| | 29/8 | | 1 O.R. proceeded on leave | |
| | 30/8 | | 2 O.R. rejoined from leave. 1 O.R. attached infantry admitted hospital 2nd Lt. Darlington proceeded to Etaples. 3 O.R. proceeded on leave. 3 officers | L.E.G. L.E.G. |
| | 31/8 | | and 94 O.R. infantry attached rejoined their battalions. 2nd Lt. Davis and servant rejoined Monmouth Regt. | L.E.G. |

J.E. Hall Major R.E.(T)
o/c 497 (Monmouth) Field Coy R.E.

Army Form C. 2118.

# WAR DIARY
## or
## INTELLIGENCE SUMMARY.
*(Erase heading not required.)*

Instructions regarding War Diaries and Intelligence Summaries are contained in F. S. Regs., Part II. and the Staff Manual respectively. Title pages will be prepared in manuscript.

| Place | Date 1917 | Hour | Summary of Events and Information | Remarks and references to Appendices |
|---|---|---|---|---|
| Pottsdown Camp PROVEN | Sept 1st | | 2 O.R. admitted Hospital. 3 O.R. rejoined from leave | A.C.1 |
| do | 2nd | | 2 O.R. proceeded on leave. 3 O.R. rejoined from leave | A.C.2 |
| do | 3rd | | 6 O.R. reinforcements joined Bty. 3 O.R. proceeded on leave | A.C.3 |
| do | 4th | | 2 O.R. proceeded on leave. 2 O.R. rejoined from leave. 1 O.R. rejoined from leave | A.C.4 |
| do | 5th | | 3 O.R. proceeded on leave. 2nd Lt Darling in rejoined from leave. 2 O.R. rejoined from leave | A.C.5 |
| do | 6th | | 2 O.R. proceeded on leave. 3 O.R. rejoined from leave | A.C.6 |
| do | 7th | | 3 O.R. proceeded on leave. 7 O.R. rejoined from leave | A.C.7 |
| do | 8th | | 2nd Lt. Darling proceeded to base. 2 O.R. proceeded on leave. 1 O.R. to 29th Div. Gas school for course. 1 O.R. rejoined from 29 Div Gas school from course | A.C.8 |
| do | 9 | | 2 O.R. proceeded on leave. 10 R rejoined to from 18th M.V.S. Prevention line. Major Capt G. RUSTON hying the company from leave & resumes command. | O.O.7/R |
| do | 10/9 | | 3 O.R. return from leave | O.O.7/R |
| | 11/9 | | 1 O.R. return from leave | O.O.7/R |
| | 12/9 | | 5 O.R. return from leave. 2 O.R. admitted Hospital | O.O.7/R |

**Army Form C. 2118.**

# WAR DIARY
## or
## INTELLIGENCE SUMMARY.
(Erase heading not required.)

Instructions regarding War Diaries and Intelligence Summaries are contained in F. S. Regs., Part II. and the Staff Manual respectively. Title pages will be prepared in manuscript.

| Place | Date | Hour | Summary of Events and Information | Remarks and references to Appendices |
|---|---|---|---|---|
| PORTSDOWN CAMP PROVEN | 1917 13/9 | | Capt. L.C.HALL & Batman go to XIV Corps Rest Station | OO/R |
| | | | 10.R. goes to XIV Corps School | |
| | | | 10.R. — 29th Divl. Gas School | |
| | | | 10.R. returns from 29th Divl. Gas School | OO/R |
| | 14/9 | | 3.O.R. return from leave | |
| | | | 1.O.R. Inoculated. Brought Dental treatment | OO/R |
| | | | 2.O.R. report from leave | OO/R |
| | 15/9 | | 1.O.R. Transferred to Depot 2nd Army 6. R.E. | |
| | 16/9 | | 2.O.R. report from leave | |
| | | | 1.O.R. rejoins from Hospital | |
| | 17/9 | | 2.O.R. return from leave | OO/R |
| | | | 2.O.R. return to duty from leave Capt. L.C.HALL & Batman return from XIV Corps Rest Station | OO/R |
| | 18/9 | | 2.O.R. 102. O.R. infantry Corps 56th Bde. attached H.Q. as carrying party. | OO/R |
| | 19/9 | | 10.R. return from leave | |
| | | | Company (less transport) moves to ELVERDINGHE | |
| EVERDINGHE | 20/9 | | Transport moves to ONDANK | OO/R |
| | | | 10.R. goes to Hospital | |
| | 21/9 | | 50.R. return to duty from leave | |
| | | | 10.R. return from Hospital | |
| | | | 10.R. rehabilitation (carrying party) admitted Hosp. wound. & 70.R. (carrying party) admitted Hosp. (Ack.) | OO/R |

# WAR DIARY
## or
## INTELLIGENCE SUMMARY.
(Erase heading not required.)

Army Form C. 2118.

| Place | Date 1917 | Hour | Summary of Events and Information | Remarks and references to Appendices |
|---|---|---|---|---|
| ELVER-DINGHE | 22/9 | | 30.R. Proceeded on leave. | |
| | | | 26.R. report from leave | |
| | | | Lt R.S. DAVIES & Batman (1/2 MON. REGT.) attached to Co. | |
| | | | 10.R. admitted Hospital (sick) | 009/R |
| | | | 10.R. (carrying party) admitted Hospital (sick) | 009/R |
| | 23/9 | | 30.R. return to duty from leave | |
| | | | H.Q.R. Reinforcing draft from Company. | |
| | 24/9 | | 30.R. return to duty from leave. | 009/R |
| | | | 10.R. att.d to M.V.S. Co. @ Elverd. | |
| | 25/9 | | 10.R. admitted Hospital sick. | |
| | | | 50.R. Reinforcing draft from Co. | |
| | | | 10.R. reports Co. from Base | |
| | 26/9 | | 10.R. (carrying party) wounded | 009/R |
| | | | 10.R. proc on leave. | |
| | 27/9 | | 10.R. proc on leave. | 009/R |
| | 28/9 | | 10.R. goes on leave | 009/R |
| | 29/9 | | 10.R. Return to unit from Hospital | |
| | | | 11 Lt A.E. NEAR proc to 5th Army School, TOUTENCOURT. (W. Autumn) | |
| | | | 10.R. wounded | 009/R |

# WAR DIARY
## INTELLIGENCE SUMMARY.
*(Erase heading not required.)*

Army Form C. 2118.

| Place | Date | Hour | Summary of Events and Information | Remarks and references to Appendices |
|---|---|---|---|---|
| ELVER - DINGHE | 29/9 | | #2/LT CHAPMAN wounded (gassed) 10.R. (carrying party) admitted hospital (sick). | |
| | 30/9 | | 10R " " " (gassed) | |

O.B.R[?]ston
Major R.E.(T)
O.C. 497ᵉ (Kent) Fld. Co. R.E.

CONFIDENTIAL.

War Diary

of

497th Kent Field Company R.E.

From 1st September, 1917 to 30th September, 1917.

VOLUME XXIV.

-*-*-*-

CONFIDENTIAL

War Diiary

of

497th (Kent) Field Company R.E.

From 1st October, 1917, to 31st October, 1917.

VOLUME XXV.

-*-*-

Vol 20

# WAR DIARY
## or
## INTELLIGENCE SUMMARY.
*(Erase heading not required.)*

Army Form C. 2118.

| Place | Date 1917 | Hour | Summary of Events and Information | Remarks and references to Appendices |
|---|---|---|---|---|
| ELVERDINGHE | 1/10 | | Strength: 60 O/R<br>1 Interpreter<br>154 Dismounted } O/Ranks<br>54 Mounted }<br>30 Officers<br>96 O/Ranks<br>Attached Infantry Carrying Party:-<br>Attached for instruction<br>10 Officers (Pioneers)<br>18 R (Batmen)<br>Attached Junior Transport<br>10 R. (Infantry) | |
| | 2/10 | | 10 R. wounded<br>10 R. (Anti-gas carrying party) wounded<br>20 R. ( " " " ) admitted Hospital sick | A/R<br>A/R<br>A/R<br>A/R |
| | 3/10<br>4/10<br>5/10 | | 10 R. rejoined company from No 54 C.C.S. (Offr Batman)<br>10 R. (Anti Inf.y carrying party) admitted Hospital (shellshock)<br>2 O.R. fr/ on leave<br>2 O.R. return from leave | A/R |

# WAR DIARY
## or
## INTELLIGENCE SUMMARY.

Army Form C. 2118.

| Place | Date 1917 | Hour | Summary of Events and Information | Remarks and references to Appendices |
|---|---|---|---|---|
| ELVERDINGHE | 4/10 | | 10R. returned from line | OC 74R |
| | 7/10 | | 173.W.A. LOWE R.E. (T.) joins company | |
| | | | 10R. rejoins from line | OC 74R |
| | 8/10 | | 10R. returns to line from line | OC 74R |
| | 9/10 | | 20R. proceed on leave | |
| | | | Company performed the following tasks during operations:— | |
| | | | (a) With 171 assistance of 409th Rly Field Co. R.E., they reinstated new track off Duinks Avenue, in PUFFS HOUSE as far as D29 V 25 & 67. to spotted the switch north with WHITE ROAD. | |
| | | | (b) Bridge on YPRES - STADEN RAILWAY at D29 V 7 d.3.8 was cleared of obstacles & allowed traffic to float on railway sleeper bridge (constructed 6" wide with sloped approaches. | |
| | | | (c) 60ˣ of runway pinned near bridge in (b) was made passable by canvas mats, planking & duckboards. | |
| | | | | OC 74R |
| | | | (d) Track constructed across marsh at V17 d.99 & BLOEMBEEK bridged with duckboards & slabs. | |
| | | | (e) Bridges at V18 C 25.80 & V12 d.75 reconnoitered & found poor. Bridge (at V16 & 2 main fine etc) Mullinsport. | |
| PROVEN | 10/10 | | Company transport move to PROVEN - PATAGONIA CAMP P5 Cam - 27/E/17 & 7.5. | |
| | 10/10 | | 10R. rejoins from C.R.S. | OC 74R |
| | | | 20R. returns from leave. | OC 74R |
| | | | 369970 & 772 DR (attached inf. Carrying Party) rejoin their units. | |
| | 11/10 | | 20R. from leave. | |

# WAR DIARY
## INTELLIGENCE SUMMARY.
*(Erase heading not required.)*

Army Form C. 2118.

| Place | Date | Hour | Summary of Events and Information | Remarks and references to Appendices |
|---|---|---|---|---|
| PROVEN | 11/10 | | 11/Lt DAVIES returned from this unit | |
| | | | 11/Lt W.H. DARLINGTON joined Company from No 3 Reinforcement. | |
| | 12/10 | | 3 O.R. (temporary draft) from Company | O.5 P.R |
| | | | 13 O.R posted to 2/Depot Army Rest Camp | O.5 P.R |
| | 13/10 | | 10 O.R. returned from XIV Battn School | |
| | 14/10 | | — | |
| | | | 1 O.R. proc. on leave to U.K. (one month) | |
| | | | 1 O.R. returned from C.R.E. | |
| | | | 1 O.R. " " Area Commandant, Proven. | |
| | 15/10 | | 1 O.R. proc. on leave to U.K. | O.5 P.R |
| | 16/10 | | 2 O.R. " " " | O.5 P.R |
| | | | 3 O.R. embks due for leave (2 on 17th + 1 on 18th) proc.d to POPERINGHE to await leave train | O.5 P.R |
| HOPOUTRE | | | Company moves by train to HOPOUTRE + entrains there | |
| BEAUMETZ RIVIERE | 17/10 | | Company proceeds by rail to BEAUMETZ-RIVIERE + detrains there | |
| BLAIREVILLE | 18/10 | | Company moves by rail to quarters in BLAIREVILLE | O.5 P.R |
| " | 19/10 | | 11/Lt W.B. Darlington proceeded to U.K. on leave. | |
| | | | 1 O.R. proceeded on leave to U.K. | |
| | | | 1 O.R. rejoined coy from leave | |

# WAR DIARY
## or
## INTELLIGENCE SUMMARY
(Erase heading not required.)

Army Form C. 2118.

| Place | Date | Hour | Summary of Events and Information | Remarks and references to Appendices |
|---|---|---|---|---|
| Pluviosa | 20/10 | | 16 O.R. proceeded to 3rd Army rest camp | A/28 |
| | 21/10 | | 2 O.R. proceeded on leave to U.K. | A/28 |
| | | | Coy moved to Bonavelle in temp. by road | |
| | | | Major A.I.G. Paston took over duties of C.R.E. 29 Div | |
| Bonavelles | 22/10 | | 2 O.R. admitted hospital | A/28 |
| | | | 1 O.R. rejoins by from leave | |
| | | | 13 O.R. rejoins by from ordinary rest camp | |
| | 23/10 | | 3 O.R. admitted hospital | A/28 |
| | 24/10 | | 2nd Lt. P. Neill joined by | A/28 |
| | | | 2 O.R. rejoined by from leave | |
| | | | 1 O.R. rejoined by from hospital | |
| | | | No. 416 section transferred to 62nd Coy. has taken Works by R.E. | |
| | 25/10 | | 2 O.R. rejoined by from leave | |
| | | | 2 O.R. proceeded to U.K. on leave | |
| | | | Coy (dismounted section) moves from Bonavelles 6 temps to be lent to chief Engineer by road and thence by rail to Fins and thence by road to Hendecourt | |

**Army Form C. 2118.**

# WAR DIARY
## or
## INTELLIGENCE SUMMARY.
*(Erase heading not required.)*

Instructions regarding War Diaries and Intelligence Summaries are contained in F. S. Regs., Part II. and the Staff Manual respectively. Title pages will be prepared in manuscript.

| Place | Date | Hour | Summary of Events and Information | Remarks and references to Appendices |
|---|---|---|---|---|
| Doncelles | 25/10 | | Transport moved by road to Henchcourt via Bapaume | |
| Henchcourt | 26/10 | | Coy dismounted and transport arrived at Henchcourt | |
| | 27/10 | | 1 O.R. proceeded on leave to U.K. | |
| | 28/10 | | Coy dismounted section moved to forward to W.S.6 | |
| W.S.6 | 29/10 | | 2 O.R. proceeded on leave to U.K. | |
| | | | 1 O.R. admitted hospital | |
| | 30/10 | | 1 O.R. admitted hospital | |
| | 31/10 | | 3 O.R. returned from leave | |

H Hall
Capt RE
OC 107th (Kent) Field Coy R.E.

CONFIDENTIAL.

WAR DIARY.

OF

497TH (KENT) FIELD COY., R.E.,

VOLUME 26.

(November 1917).

Army Form C. 2118.

# WAR DIARY
## or
## INTELLIGENCE SUMMARY.
*(Erase heading not required.)*

Instructions regarding War Diaries and Intelligence Summaries are contained in F.S. Regs., Part II. and the Staff Manual respectively. Title pages will be prepared in manuscript.

| Place | Date 1917 | Hour | Summary of Events and Information | Remarks and references to Appendices |
|---|---|---|---|---|
| W 56 | | | | |
| Army Command | 1/11 | | 1 O.R. admitted hospital sick | A1/16 |
| | | | 1 O.R. rejoined from leave | 1/16 |
| do | 2/11 | | 1 O.R. transferred to 570 (London Field Coy) R.E. | |
| do | 3/11 | | 1 O.R. admitted to hospital sick | AIII/16 |
| Field to Gond | | | Coy dismounted section moved to Gondé to Gond | HI/16 |
| | | | 15 O.R. rejoined Coy from III Army rest camp | |
| | 4/11 | | 2 O.R. reinforcing draft joined Coy | AIV/16 |
| | 5/11 | | 4 O.R. rejoined Coy from leave | |
| | 6/11 | | 2 O.R. rejoined from hospital | |
| | | | 1 O.R. rejoined by from leave | |
| | | | 1 O.R. proceeded on leave | |
| | | | 1 Lt. F. NEAL and 1 O.R. rejoined Coy from Wimy School | |
| | 7/11 | | 3 O.R. rejoined Coy from leave | AV/16 |
| | 8/11 | | 2 O.R. proceeded on leave | |
| | 9/11 | | 6 O.R. rejoined Coy from 86°Bgd H.Q. | AVI/16 |
| | | | 3 O.R. proceeded on leave | AVII/16 |
| | 10/11 | | 1 Lt. W.E. DARLINGTON rejoined Coy from leave | |
| | 12/11 | | 3 O.R. proceeded on leave | |

# WAR DIARY
## or
## INTELLIGENCE SUMMARY.
*(Erase heading not required.)*

Army Form C. 2118.

| Place | Date 1917 | Hour | Summary of Events and Information | Remarks and references to Appendices |
|---|---|---|---|---|
| SOREL-LE-GRAND | 12/11 | | MAJOR A.F.G. RUSTON assumes Co. on return of Lt.Col. H. BIDDULPH, DSO, R.E., G.R.E. 10R. (Batmn) returns Co. Attended conference (with CRE.) as to accommodation in camping areas, present - representatives of G.H.Q. + CRE's of 6th, 12th, 20th + 29th Divns + representative of Corps. Visited works and sites of proposed camps in DESSART WOOD + on FINS-NEUVILLE Road. | O97R |
| | 13/11 | | Visited (w. CRE) EQUANCOURT, MANANCOURT, + NURLU. Company employed: 2½ sections puncturing huts at NURLU. 1½ sections completing camouflage screening of huts at GREAT SOREL + preparing timber work for camouflaged camp. | O97R |
| | 14/11 | | 3 O.R. from leave. 2 O.R. attached III Corps for Training. Visited (w. AAAA Adjt. R.E.) VILLERS PLOUICH, BEAUCAMP + QUEENS CROSS. ~~BAAAAAAAAAAAAAAA~~ Company employed: 1 section on camouflaged camp on FINS - NEUVILLE BOURJONVAL Road 1 Company area Bourjonval camp. | O97R |
| | 15/11 | | Visited following works in morning:- Erection of YMCA HUT FINS; camouflaged camps; north of Puisieux in DESSART WOOD + in making camouflaged screens between tarpaulins in FINS. 3 the last work referred to mentioned | O97R |
| | | 5.30 p.m. | Attended (w. CRE) G.O.C. conference of CRE's of 1st, 12th, 20th, 29th + 40th Divns. at SOREL. Company employed; 2 sections at NCO's + men's autumn puncturing drill, small party assisting in erection of YMCA HUT FINS. Party helping autumn at SOREL CAMPS. Remd floor, setting of camouflaged camp. (3 completed) (½ completed) | O97R |

A 58.14  Wt. W4973/M687  750,000  8/16  D. D. & L. Ltd.  Forms/C.2118/13

# WAR DIARY
## INTELLIGENCE SUMMARY.
*(Erase heading not required.)*

Army Form C. 2118.

Instructions regarding War Diaries and Intelligence Summaries are contained in F. S. Regs., Part II. and the Staff Manual respectively. Title pages will be prepared in manuscript.

| Place | Date 1917 | Hour | Summary of Events and Information | Remarks and references to Appendices |
|---|---|---|---|---|
| SOREL-LE-GRAND | 16/11 | | 1 O.R. admitted Hospital (sick) | |
| | | | 3 O.R. for Leave | |
| | | | 1 O.R. Returns to duty from Bombing School. | |
| | | Morn. | Visited (w. CRE, O.C. Pulham RE) GOUZEAUCOURT + point where 15 RAVINE CROSS GOUZEAUCOURT — VILLERS PLOUICH ROAD. | |
| | | Aft. | Pro.d (w. Capt. HALL RE) Camouflaged Camp (FINS). Camouflaged Mule Standings (FINS) YMCA HUT (FINS) + enclosure of Blankets into FINS + SOREL. | |
| | | | Company employed:— | |
| | | | 1 Offr. + 2 O.R. (2 NH. + 4 Dn.) reconnoitring forward tracks thru Ja. | |
| | | | 6 O.R. assist in erection of YMCA HUT (entrance ended + party walled) | |
| | | | 1 section bring back Pontoons + trestles from MANANCOURT. | |
| | | | 1 section entirely camouflaged camp (work completed except for fastening &c. of obliterating sheets) | ⊘R |
| | | | 1 section each erect Blanket Dump at SOREL + FINS. | |
| | 17/11 | | 8 O.R. for Leave. | |
| | | | 2 O.R. Return from Leave. | |
| | | Morn. | Visited works on Camouflaged Waggon Standings, ReinforceD + Pack Sites at GOUZEAUCOURT, FINS + SOREL. | |
| | | O.E. | C.R.E. in person. S.S.O. + 2nd in command attended Impending situation + tasks of Field Co. sketched out. | |
| | | | Company employed:— No. 1 Sect : Pack Site Equipment (1 [?] + 3 at [?]) | |
| | | | 2 : Drawing Camouflaged Lamp [?] Improving D.A.D.O.S site. | |
| | | | 3 : Gathering brush, erecting Dug-outs Dump — R[?] | |
| | | | 4 : Improving Mule Stabling [?] GR. Camp Dump. 1 pack store erected [?] Railway Matn.... | ⊘R |
| | | | Working Parties on Newfoundland Road (labour provided J. 2 of [?]) | |

# WAR DIARY
## INTELLIGENCE SUMMARY.
*(Erase heading not required.)*

Army Form C. 2118.

| Place | Date 1917 | Hour | Summary of Events and Information | Remarks and references to Appendices |
|---|---|---|---|---|
| SOREL-LE-GRAND | 18/5 | | 10 R. admitted Hospital (sick). 10 R. returned to duty from leave. | O.C./R L.N.S |
| | 19/5 | | 2nd Lieut HART & 2nd Lts. A.P. NEAL & P. NEILL attached. 2nd Lts NEAL & P. NEILL reconnoitred roads & tracks round GOUZEAUCOURT. Joined as C.R.E. Companies employed: Sect.1: Shelters at EQUANCOURT (H finished except banco) 2: Plateau Posts & recceing Sect 3. 3: Shelters @ C.R.E. HQ & (Shelter, latrines, bathhouse & platforms on Neech Plateau completed) + Pack Sheds @ SOREL; 3 completed (rest new on) 4. Corstacks for FINS; 3 completed (inclarced) accept camouflage | L.N.S |
| | 20/5 | | Reconnoitred section of Company. Moved to Gouzeaucourt. | L.N.S |
| | 21/5 | | Company moved to bivouacs. Hostile batlie wounded 1 man. Bivouac Killein Plaid. | L.N.S |
| | 24/5 | | Transport wounded Lt R.B.G.S., Lieut S.T.B. 1 Officer (M.V.R. Goddard) wounded. 2 O.Rks wounded. | L.N.S |
| | 26/5 | | I.O.R. admitted hospital, sick. | L.N.S |

Army Form C. 2118.

# WAR DIARY
## or
## INTELLIGENCE SUMMARY.
*(Erase heading not required.)*

Instructions regarding War Diaries and Intelligence Summaries are contained in F.S. Regs., Part II. and the Staff Manual respectively. Title pages will be prepared in manuscript.

| Place | Date | Hour | Summary of Events and Information | Remarks and references to Appendices |
|---|---|---|---|---|
| Rem H.Q. | 27/5 | | 2. O. R's rejoined Coy. from the leave. 2.O.R's. went on leave. | Appx. |
| P. & B.G. | 29/5 | | 2. O. R's returned from leave. 1. O. R. went on leave. | RAZ |
| | 30/5 | | 3 Officers, Prisoners of War, being: A. & G. Rawlin. Capt. L. C. Hill. Lieut. A. F. Ned. " P. Hill. " W. A. Lowe. | |
| | | | 8 7. O. R's. Prisoners of War. 2. O. R's wounded. Transport to hand. | Appx. |

Mitchell
Lieut. R.S.

497 (km) HC Coy R.S.

CONFIDENTIAL

WAR DIARY

OF

497TH (KENT) FD. Co RE

1/12/17 to 31/12/17

VOLUME XXVII

Army Form C. 2118.

# WAR DIARY
# of
# INTELLIGENCE SUMMARY

(Erase heading not required.)

Instructions regarding War Diaries and Intelligence Summaries are contained in F. S. Regs., Part II. and the Staff Manual respectively. Title pages will be prepared in manuscript.

| Place | Date | Hour | Summary of Events and Information | Remarks and references to Appendices |
|---|---|---|---|---|
| India | 1/1/17 | | 1. O. R. unaltered. | |
| Bombay | 1/1/17 | | Rein H.Q. & Transport moved to Deol. to Grenadier. | MM |
| Deol. to Grenadier. 2/1/17 | | | 3. O. Rs. rejoined Coy from leave. Transport & Rein H.Q. moved to Grenadier Camp. near Deol. | MM |
| | 3/1/17 | | 3. O. Rs. rejoined Coy from leave. 2. O. Rs. rejoined Coy from TT Corps Receiving Station. 2. O. Rs. joined Coy (reinforcements) | MM |
| | 4/1/17 | | 2. O. Rs. proceed on leave. | MM |
| | 5/1/17 | | Transport moved by road to Bapaume. Rein H.Q. entrained at 2 Lieuvent. 2. O. Rs. joined Coy (reinforcements) 1. O. R. rejoin from hospital. 2. O. Rs. rejoined from leave. | MM |
| | 6/1/17 | | Rein H.Q. detrained at Edw Amiens. & proceeded to Grovesen Casern. | MM |

# WAR DIARY
## or
## INTELLIGENCE SUMMARY

Army Form C. 2118.

*(Erase heading not required.)*

Instructions regarding War Diaries and Intelligence Summaries are contained in F. S. Regs., Part II. and the Staff Manual respectively. Title pages will be prepared in manuscript.

| Place | Date | Hour | Summary of Events and Information | Remarks and references to Appendices |
|---|---|---|---|---|
| Behencourt | 7/12/17 | | Run H.Q. arrived Behencourt. Transport arrived. Behencourt. 7. O.R.s rejoined from leave. 1.O.R. rejoined from hospital. | AA/ |
| | 8/12/17 | | 1.O.R. rejoined from leave. Capt. H.W. Wetelia R.E. joins Company. Hilton men Command. | AAA |
| BERLENCOURT | 9/12/17 | | One O.R. adm. to Hospital sick | AAA |
| " | 10/12/17 | | LT. F.O. CLEVELY, LT. A.D. MCLEISH & 111 J.B.S. ALLAN joins R.E. Coy from the Base | AAA |
| " | 11/12/17 | | One O.R. proceeds on leave to U.K. | AA |
| " | 12/12/17 | | One O.R. proceeds on leave to U.K. 91. O.R. Dismounted & 1 O.R. mounted joined Coy as reinforcements from Base about 55% of some having never served a thies Coy in France; remainder having never served in R.E. training Depots at home and in France, to PIONEER UNITS; serving in some find about 3 months instruction | AAA |
| | | | reported to this Coy. | |
| | 13/12/17 | | One O.R. proceed on leave to U.K. | AAA |
| | 14/12/17 | | One O.R. return to duty from III Corps School | AAA |
| | 15/12/17 | | Four O.R. Return to duty from leave to U.K. Capt. G.E. LINES R.E. joins Coy or Sec in Command. | AAA |
| | 16/12/17 | | Company moved by roads to AUBROMETZ. Mulen horse supplied 86th Brigade for Blankets and Musipacks | AAA RE |

Murrochler Major

# WAR DIARY
## or
## INTELLIGENCE SUMMARY.
(Erase heading not required.)

Army Form C. 2118.

| Place | Date | Hour | Summary of Events and Information | Remarks and references to Appendices |
|---|---|---|---|---|
| TUBROMETZ | 17/12/17 | | One O.R. rejoins Coy from Hospital | — |
| " | " | | O.R. " " " leave | — |
| " | " | | One O.R. proceeds on Leave | — |
| BERLENCOURT | 18/12/17 | | Company moved by road to BERLENCOURT. | — |
| " | " | | Company arrives by road at GOURNAY. Heavy fall of snow, newton hem fails to meet BERLENCOURT convoys at crossroads | — |
| " | " | | Lorries spend night of 18-15 nut at crossroads or crossroads | — |
| GOURNAY | 19/12/17 | | Sent two Peeler lorries back to BERLENCOURT for Blankets & Packs. | — |
| " | 20/12/17 | | Blankets & Packs arrive | — |
| " | 21/12/17 | | Black L.D. Mare (age) knocked by convoy nr Lt. shot | — |
| " | " | | Two O.R. proceed on leave to U.K. | — |
| " | 23/12/17 | | Two O.R. proceed on leave to U.K. | — |
| " | " | | One O.R. returns to BnS from leave U.K. | — |
| " | " | | One O.R. proceeds to join Depot with Sunda Coy for transfer. | — |
| " | 24/12/17 | | Two O.R. join Coy as reinforcements from Base | — |
| " | 25/12/17 | | C.R.E. visits Coy & inspects various items to M.K. | — |
| " | " | | Lt S.A. Smutt proceeds on leave to U.K. | — |
| " | 26/12/17 | | One O.R. admitted to Hospital Sick | — |
| " | 27/12/17 | | One L.B. getting in Ambulance kicked on stifle. shot | — |
| " | 28/12/17 | | One O.R. joins Coy Reinforcement | — |
| " | 29/12/17 | | One O.R. returns from leave U.K. | — |
| " | 30/12/17 | | One O.R. " to duty from 18th M.V.S | — |
| " | 31/12/17 | | One O.R. " from leave U.K. | — |

CONFIDENTIAL.

WAR DIARY

of

497th (Kent) Field Coy R.E.

From 1st January 1918 to 31st January 1918.

VOLUME XXVIII

# WAR DIARY
## or
## INTELLIGENCE SUMMARY.

Army Form C. 2118.

Volume No. XXVII

| Place | Date | Hour | Summary of Events and Information | Remarks and references to Appendices |
|---|---|---|---|---|
| WIZERNES GOURNEY. | 1/1/18 | | 1. O.R. leave to U.K. | |
| | | | 2. O.R. return to duty from leave | |
| | | | 1. O.R. " " from base CRE | |
| | | | 2. O.R. join Coy from R.E. Base Depôt | |
| " | 2/1/18 | | 1. O.R. leave to U.K. | |
| | 3/1/18 | | 1/Lt G.E. Felwitt joins Coy | |
| | 4/1/18 | | Coy moved by road to WIZERNES | |
| WIZERNES | | | 6 O.R. admit to Hospital. Sick | |
| | | | Leave U.K. | |
| | 5.1.18 | | " return to duty from Hospital | |
| | 6.1.18 | | Two O.R. return to duty from leave | |
| | | | One " adm. Hospital Sick | |
| | 7.1.18 | | " " leave to U.K. | |
| | | | " return to duty from leave | |
| | 8.1.18 | | Transferred to G.H.Q. | |
| | 9.1.18 | | Admit to Hospital | |
| | 10.1.18 | | Attached B.H.Q. for duty | |
| | 11.1.18 | | M. Horan rejoins Coy from leave | |
| | | | Lt. Smith rejoins Coy from leave | |
| | | | " S.A. Smith transferred to Central Purchase Board autouts A.G/55/634 (c) | |
| | 12/1/18 | | Two O.R. leave to U.K. | |
| | | | One O.R. adm Hospital Sick | |
| | 13/1/18 | | " return to duty from leave | |
| | 14/1/18 | | Two " leave to U.K. | |
| | 15/1/18 | | One " adm Hospital Sick | |
| | | | Mounted Section under Capt Horn proceeded by road to Ypres area stopping at ZERMEZELLE night 15/16th arriving BRANDHOECK 16th noon | |
| | 16/1/18 | | Coy + Officers Dugout in Q.S.W. & Welsh cart proceed by rail to BRANDHOECK and marched from there to billets at LOCK GATE YPRES | |

497TH (KENT) FIELD CO: R.E.

Amichle Major O.C.

# WAR DIARY
## or
## INTELLIGENCE SUMMARY.
*(Erase heading not required.)*

Army Form C. 2118.

| Place | Date | Hour | Summary of Events and Information | Remarks and references to Appendices |
|---|---|---|---|---|
| YPRES | 17.11.18 | | Coy working on Coy Billets | Nil |
| | 18.11.18 | | " | |
| | 19.11.18 | | Took men from 15th YEO Coy. to Fin Musse Area work | |
| | 20.11.18 | | Tape out GRAVENSTAFEL Defensive Position | |
| | | | Two sections working on this — about 500 infantry | |
| | | | Lt Gallagher + 1 Cerb and 1 O.R attached 465 Yeoman for duty | |
| | | | One O.R attached C.R.E for duty | |
| | 21.11.18 | | One O.R attached 2nd Lt Bn. Signal Co. for duty | |
| | | | returns from leave | |
| | | | Two ? Hospital ? sick | |
| | 22.11.18 | | Two Sections Gravenstafel Defensive line | |
| | 23.11.18 | | Two O.R. return to duty from leave | |
| | 24.11.18 | | One O.R. leave to U.K | |
| | | | One O.R. return duty from Hospital | |
| | 25.11.18 | | One O.R. leave to U.K | |
| | 26.11.18 | | Three O.R. 103 O.R infantry on 85 Bgde attached for duty rations | |
| | | | Lt Adolph Burnett + 1 O.R report for duty from 447 Coy | |
| | | | Took men forwards work from ore near ? 1 N.CO | |
| | 27.11.18 | | Two sections working on GOURBERG check point work — in ? officers + 1 N.CO | |
| | | | inspection G.T. (on O.R. Sunning) G.T.P. in PASSCHENDAELE | |
| | | | Two O.R. leave U.K | |
| | 28.11.18 | | One O.R. report for leave | |
| | | | Some as 27th ? work on O.R. Sch. for repair of ? GOURBERG TRACK | |
| | | | One O.R to VIII Corps Bn School — completion. | |
| | 29.11.18 | | Two Sections working BELLE VUE defence line | |
| | 30.11.18 | | American officer & one O.R. attached for instruction | |
| | 31.11.18 | | Two sections working BELLE VUE defence line | |
| | | | One O.R leave to U.K | |

Mmehta Maj RE for O.C.
497th (KENT) FIELD CO: R.E.

CONFIDENTIAL.

WAR DIARY

of

497th (Kent) Field Coy R.E.

From 1/2/18 to 28/2/18.

VOLUME No. XXIX.

Army Form C. 2118.

# WAR DIARY
## — or —
## INTELLIGENCE SUMMARY.
*(Erase heading not required.)*

Instructions regarding War Diaries and Intelligence Summaries are contained in F. S. Regs., Part II. and the Staff Manual respectively. Title pages will be prepared in manuscript.

| Place | Date | Hour | Summary of Events and Information | Remarks and references to Appendices |
|---|---|---|---|---|
| YPRES | 1/2/18 | | Cpl Pope and 4 OR wounded. One OR reformed from leave to U.K. | |
| | 2-2-18 | | One OR transferred to 2/1st Bn Devon Co. RE. Company missing BELLE VUE dugout line. Two OR proceed on leave to U.K. | Jmm |
| | 3-2-18 | | One OR rejoined by from leave. Co. missing BELLE VUE dugout line. One officer and 33 OR Cots reported their unit One O.R. reported from Gas School. Hard night of work on forward area to date. Dugouts & 5'10' tall by RE Completed. Dugouts forward area under 5'10'15 field On we work on Bn. Reserve line Work on unable are work from 5'10'15 field On D7 and 76. | |
| | 4-2-18 | | Two OR rejoined Co. from leave to U.K. One officer to 34 OR at No.1 Bn & reported their unit One officer to 34 OR 2nd Field Bn & reported to U.K. Capt. hunro taken over command of Co Major Meletz proceeds on leave to U.K. | Imraki |
| ,, | 5-2-18 | | | |
| ,, | 6-2-18 | | 1 O.R. proceeded on leave to U.K. Company working on Divisional Reserve Line GRAVENSTAFEL One section at night with about 300 2ft; three sections by day with 100 2ft. | |
| ,, | 7-2-18 | | nothing to report. work continued. | |
| | 8-2-18 | | Sgt. Whyte J. proceeded to 4th Army school for Course of Instruction. work continued. | |
| | 9-2-18 | | 1 O.R. admitted Hospital. 1 O.R. joined Co. from 94s RE Ankyon Co. 1 O.R. rejoined Co. from leave to U.K. | H.H. |
| | 10-2-18 | | 4 O.R. proceeded on leave to U.K. Handed over work on Divisional Reserve Line to 1 O.R. admitted to Hospital. 490 F.Co. R.E. | |

# WAR DIARY
## or
## INTELLIGENCE SUMMARY.

Army Form C. 2118.

| Places | Date | Hour | Summary of Events and Information | Remarks and references to Appendices |
|---|---|---|---|---|
| YPRES | 11-2-18 | | Moved into WEBSTER CAMP. Handed over LOCK GATE CAMP to 15 F.C. R.E. Took over work on Army Battle Zone. | |
| " | 12-2-18 | | Commenced work on Army Battle Zone. LIEUT. FINNEGAN R.E. (A.B.Z.) attached to Coy. LON, SQUARE KEEPS. VIII Corps. work on GREY, RUPPRECHT. | |
| " | 13-2-18 | | 1 O.R. admitted to Hospital. 1 O.R. rejoined Coy. from leave. | |
| " | 14-2-18 | | 1 O.R. leave to U.K. | |
| " | 15-2-18 | | 2 O.R. rejoined from leave to U.K. | J.F. |
| " | 16-2-18 | | 1/Cpl. Carle e. proceeded to Bridging School AIRE. 1 O.R. rejoined from leave to U.K. | |
| " | 17-2-18 | | 1 O.R. admitted Hospital. 1 O.R. rejoined from leave. | |
| " | 18-2-18 | | 2 O.R. admitted Hospital. 3 O.R. proceeded on leave to U.K. | |
| " | 19-2-18 | | 1 O.R. admitted Hospital. 1 O.R. rejoined from leave. 1 O.R. rejoined from Hospital. | |
| " | 20-2-18 | | 1 O.R. rejoined from Hospital. Capt [?] took over command of Coy. | J.F. Weir Capt R.E. |
| " | 21-2-18 | | 6 O.R. rejoined Coy. from leave to U.K. and took over command of Coy. | |
| " | 22-2-18 | | 1 O.R. rejoined Coy. from Hospital | |
| " | 23-2-18 | | Two O.R. rejoined Coy. from R.E. Base Depot | |
| " | 24-2-18 | | Two O.R. proceeded on leave to U.K. | |
| " | 25-2-18 | | 6 O.R. admitted Hospital | |
| " | 26-2-18 | | 1 Hauer [?] and 3 O.R. proceeded to R.E. Base Depot. 1 O.R. admitted to Hospital. 2 O.R. proceeded on leave to U.K. Two O.R. rejoined Coy. from leave to U.K. | |
| " | | | Major White & Lt. Rolph & 4 O.R. proceeded to LGS Pinfrying school AIRE. 6 O.R. proceeded from R.E. Base Depot. | |
| " | 28-2-18 | | 6 O.R. proceeded on leave to U.K. C.R.E. Sgt Richardson & proceeded 15 No.73 Veterinary Hospital for [?] | Munchle[?] map [?] |

CONFIDENTIAL

WAR DIARY.

of

497th (Kent) Field Coy., R.E.

From 1/3/18. To 31/3/18.

VOLUME No. 30

Army Form C. 2118.

# WAR DIARY
# INTELLIGENCE SUMMARY.

(Erase heading not required.)

Instructions regarding War Diaries and Intelligence Summaries are contained in F. S. Regs., Part II. and the Staff Manual respectively. Title pages will be prepared in manuscript.

| Place | Date | Hour | Summary of Events and Information | Remarks and references to Appendices |
|---|---|---|---|---|
| YPRES | 1/3/18 | | Company employed on Army Battle Zone. RUPPRECHT, GREY, SQUARE, LOW, BORRY KEEPS worked upon. Revetting and draining pits and constructing small concrete shelters. | M. |
| " | 2/3/18 | | 1 O.R. adm. Hospital sick. 1 O.R. retd. to duty from leave. Work as above contd. | M. |
| " | 3/3/18 | | Work as above contd. | M. |
| " | 4/3/18 | | 1 O.R. proceeded on leave to U.K. 1 O.R. retd. to duty from Hospital. | M. |
| " | 5/3/18 | | 1 O.R. adm. Hospital sick. 8 O.R. certified unfit transferred to Base Authority N.D.M.S. 29 Div. 2 O.R. retd. to duty from leave. | M. |
| " | 6/3/18 | | 1 O.R. retd. to duty from leave. 1 O.R. retd. to duty from BRIDGING SCHOOL. N° 3 t/4 section moved to SOMME DUGOUTS. | M. |
| " | 7/3/18 | | Major H.N.WEBSTER R.E. I/c Divisional School } Capt. G.E.LINES R.E. assumed command of forward LT. D. GILLESPIE R.E. Asstg } sections. Work commenced in Rt. sector of Div. front, relieving 8th Div. R.E. | M. |
| " | 8/3/18 | | 2 O.R. joined. Work on MOSSELMARKT POSTS 1-6 - PASCHENDAELE R.A. C.T. - ABRAHAM HTS. C.T. - WATERLOO-KRONPRINZ LINE - GAS PROTECTION ETC. Continued. | M. |
| " | 9/3/18 | | LT. F.D. CLEVELY wounded, adm. hospital. 1 O.R. adm. hosp. sick. Work as usual. | M. |
| " | 10/3/18 | | 1 O.R. adm. hosp. sick, 1 O.R. joined, 1 O.R. retd. to duty from hospital. Work contd. | M. |
| " | 11/3/18 | | 1 O.R. Retd. to duty from leave. Work contd. | M. |
| " | | | 1 O.R. " " " N°22 Vet. hosp. N° 2 section relieved N° 3. | M. |
| " | 12/3/18 | | 2 O.R. joined. Work contd. | M. |
| " | 13/3/18 | | 1 O.R. adm. hosp.sick. 4 O.R. transfd. Foreney Base Depot. 2/Lt. B.S. ALLAN R.E. retd. to duty from leave. 2 O.R. retd. to duty from leave. Work contd. | M. |

Army Form C. 2118

# WAR DIARY
## or
## INTELLIGENCE SUMMARY
*(Erase heading not required.)*

Instructions regarding War Diaries and Intelligence Summaries are contained in F.S. Regs., Part II. and the Staff Manual respectively. Title Pages will be prepared in manuscript.

| Place | Date | Hour | Summary of Events and Information | Remarks and references to Appendices |
|---|---|---|---|---|
| YPRES | 14/3/18 | | Personal sections moved back to YPRES on being relieved by 510 Fd. R.E. | |
| " | 15/3/18 | | Work on Brigade & Divl. horse standings commenced. Also S.T. Team dressing station, Gas protection training of P. Boxes in forward area carried on as usual. | |
| " | 16/3/18 | | 3 O.R. adm. hosp. sick. 2 O.R. transferred to POPERAY BASE DEPOT. 10 O.R. proceeded on leave to U.K. | |
| " | 17/3/18 | | 2 O.R. retd. to duty from leave. 1 O.R. attd. C.R.E. 29 Div. 10 O.R. retd. to duty from C.R.E. 29 Div. | |
| " | 18/3/18 | | LT. P.D. M'LEISH R.E. proceeded on leave to U.K. | |
| " | 19/3/18 | | 1 O.R. adm. hosp. (shell shock) 10 O.R. retd. to duty from 4th Army School. | |
| " | 20/3/18 | | 1 O.R. leave to U.K. 10 O.R. retd. to duty from hosp. | |
| " | 21/3/18 | | 1 O.R. adm. hosp. sick. | |
| " | 22/3/18 | | 1 O.R. to school of cookery. 1 O.R. to 4th Army school. 2 O.R. retd. to duty from leave. Nos. 2 & 3 sections moved to SOMME DUGOUTS, in afternoon to relieve 455 F.C.R.E. in LEFT sector of Divl. Front. | |
| " | 23/3/18 | | Work in left sector commenced. WALLEMOLEN – INCH HOUSES LINE, DIVL. RES. LINE, VENTURE F.M. C.T. to front line. Gas protection etc. 10 O.R. retd. to duty from VIII Corps Gas school. | |
| " | 24/3/18 | | 11 O.R. joined. 1 O.R. to VIII Corps. Sanitation school. Work carried on. | |
| " | 25/3/18 | | Major H.W. WEBSTER R.E. assumed command of Coy. Work carried on. LT. F.D. CLEVELY retd. to duty from Hospital. 1 O.R. retd. to duty from hosp. Work carried on. | |

Army Form C. 2118

# WAR DIARY
## or
## INTELLIGENCE SUMMARY
*(Erase heading not required.)*

Instructions regarding War Diaries and Intelligence Summaries are contained in F. S. Regs, Part II. and the Staff Manual respectively. Title Pages will be prepared in manuscript.

| Place | Date | Hour | Summary of Events and Information | Remarks and references to Appendices |
|---|---|---|---|---|
| YPRES | 26/3/18 | | 1 O.R. retd. to duty from O/C A.B.Z. VIII Corps. Lower Ants. WIELTJEMOLEN - INCH-HOUSES. HING and DIV.RESERVE LINE Gas [nuisance] from S&E Rgte | Imm |
| " | 27/3/18 | | 1 O.R. adm. hosp. sick. 1 O.R. retd. to duty from hosp. nmsk a for 26-3-18 | Imm |
| " | 28/3/18 | | 1 O.R. retd. to duty from 4th Army school. nmsk a for 27.3-18 Gas [nuisance] from machine gun arty | |
| " | 29/3/18 | | 1 O.R. adm. hosp. sick. nmsk a for 28 | |
| " | 30/3/18 | | 1 O.R. adm. hosp. sick. 1 O.R. retd. to duty from VIII Corps. Sanitation school. | |
| " | 31/3/18 | | nmsk a for 30.3. mr. | |

[signature]
O/C 157 [illegible]

29th Divisional Engineers
----------

497th (Kent) FIELD COMPANY R.E.

APRIL 1918.

CONFIDENTIAL

WAR DIARY.

of

497 (Kent) Fa Co, RE

From 1/4/18 to 30/4/18.

VOLUME No.

497 FCRE

Army Form C. 2118.

# WAR DIARY
## INTELLIGENCE SUMMARY.
(Erase heading not required.)

Instructions regarding War Diaries and Intelligence Summaries are contained in F. S. Regs., Part II. and the Staff Manual respectively. Title pages will be prepared in manuscript.

| Place | Date | Hour | Summary of Events and Information | Remarks and references to Appendices |
|---|---|---|---|---|
| Willop Camp Oak. | 1/4/18 | | 4. O.R. Reinforcement joined Company | M. |
| " | 2/4/18 | | LIEUT. J.D. MºLEISH returns Company from leave | |
| " | 3/4/18 | | 1. O.R. Returns Company from leave | |
| " | 4/4/18 | | 1. O.R. Admitted Hospital N.Y.D. Gas | |
| " | | | 1. O.R. rejoins Company from Lewis Gun School | |
| " | 5/4/18 | | 1. O.R. Admitted Hospital sick | |
| " | | | 1. O.R. rejoins Company from leave | |
| " | 6/4/18 | | 1. O.R. rejoins Company from leave | |
| " | 7/4/18 | | 2. O.R. Admitted Hospital sick | |
| " | | | 6. O.R. (Reinforcements) join Company | |
| " | 9/4/18 | | Company (Reinforcements Sickness) move to ST. JAN. TER. BIEZEN. Transport by Road. | |
| ST. JAN TER. BIEZEN | 10/4/18 | | Company (Reinforcements Sickness) less 'B' team and H.Q. Embus at PROVEN - POPERINGHE ROAD and detrus on BAILLEUL - ARMENTIERES road. 2 mile S.E. of BAILLEUL. March 2 miles to point opposite 1 mile N. of LA CRECHE and dug H. boch (each about 50% dunick) astride the main road facing S.E. during the night. When dug a sundry group of 1. N.C.O. and 4 Sabbers was detailed for each boch. The remainder of the Company rested till "Stand to" at 4 am 11th inst. Transport 'B' team & H.Q. move by road to 3/4 mile S. of R. of CROIX de POPERINGHE | W. |
| | 11/4/18 | | Company "Stood to" from 4 am - 6am Sundry Groups remained in boches all day. Remainder of Company rested till 12 noon at 68." Bde. H.Q. (form off main road 400 N. of first G. in LA CRECHE | |
| | | 12 noon | Company "Stood to" till 11.50 pm | |
| | | 11.50 pm | Company moves to reinforce 2ND HANTS REGT. in front line and came under command of O.C. 2ND HANTS REGT. Dispositions from the right and - Nº1 Section astride W. boy 2ND HANTS. | |
| | | | Nº 2 " " Z " | |
| | | | Nº 3 " " Y " | |
| | | | Nº 3 " " X " | |
| | | | All Sections dug new boches in front line linking up with infantry boches where possible. | |

A 5834. Wt. W4973/M687 750,000 8/16 D. D. & L. Ltd. Forms/C.2118/13.

**Army Form C. 2118.**

# WAR DIARY
## or
## INTELLIGENCE SUMMARY.
*(Erase heading not required.)*

Instructions regarding War Diaries and Intelligence Summaries are contained in F. S. Regs., Part II. and the Staff Manual respectively. Title pages will be prepared in manuscript.

| Place | Date | Hour | Summary of Events and Information | Remarks and references to Appendices |
|---|---|---|---|---|
| Near BAILLEUL | 12/4 | 4 am | Stood to in front line till 6 a.m. and held post during the day. Between 4.0 p.m and 5.0 p.m enemy attacked Hants Sector. Posts on left of Hants Sector and certain infantry posts on the right itself were driven back. Sections 3 and 4 were isolated and suffered casualties before falling back. Portions of them, together with parties of Hants from the same part of the trenches were rallied by Major H.W. WEBSTER R.E and returned to the trenches. No 3 Section reinforcing W Coy and No 4 Section, Z Company. MAJOR H.W. WEBSTER R.E was slightly wounded at this time (Bullet wound in Stomach) and was taken to an A.D.S. | M. |
| | 13/4 | | During the night 12/13 April No 1 and 3 Sections dug new trenches in Close Support of W Coy in order to deepen the defence. Sections 2 and 4 improved the trenches they were holding. | M. |
| Near BAILLEUL | | 1 pm | Company transport lines moved to 1/2 mile S.E of BERTHEN. Enemy attacked about 9.0 a.m but were repulsed on Hants Sector. Enemy shelled the activity at intervals during the day. | M. |
| | | 11.50 p | Orders were received from Hants Company Commander to prepare to withdraw. | |
| Near BAILLEUL | 14/4 | 12.10 am | Withdrew with Hants to new position about 600x N. of LA LEUTHE Dispositions from the right were as follows :— N.1 Section and N.3 Section with W Coy. 2nd Hants. | |
| | | | No 2 " " Z " No 4 " " X " | M. |
| | | | Sections dug themselves in before dawn and occupied the trenches all day. This position was heavily shelled at intervals during day and evening. At night N.1 Section dug his new post in this Section. | |
| | | 6.30 am | Company transport lines moved, in consequence of shelling to road junction at pt of E of BOESCHEPE. | |
| Near BAILLEUL | 15/4 | | About 1.30 am Lt. D. GILLESPIE R.E. received orders that 88th Infantry Bde would be relieved during the night (i.e. 14/15) Between 3.0 a.m and 4. a.m the relief took place and Sections fell back in rear of the Companies to which they were attached. Owing to parties of German coming up behind and working the H Sections were called together, and the Infantry | M. |

A 5832 Wt. W4973/M687 750,000 8/16 J.D.&L.Ltd Forms/C.2118/13.

Army Form C. 2118.

# WAR DIARY
## of
## INTELLIGENCE SUMMARY.
(Erase heading not required.)

Instructions regarding War Diaries and Intelligence Summaries are contained in F. S. Regs., Part II. and the Staff Manual respectively. Title pages will be prepared in manuscript.

| Place | Date | Hour | Summary of Events and Information | Remarks and references to Appendices |
|---|---|---|---|---|
| BOESCHEPE | 15/4 | | Officers having been consulted, marched back as a Company to Liangford lines near BOESCHEPE, arriving about 9 am. Casualties during period 10th–15th April KILLED 2. O.R. / DIED OF WOUNDS 1. O.R. / WOUNDED 1 Officer + 11. O.R. / WOUNDED AND MISSING / BELIEVED P.O.W. } 2. O.R. / MISSING 2. O.R. Sent to Hospital 2. O.R. | M. |
| " | 16/4 | | Company resting. 1. O.R. rejoins Company from School of Cookery. | M. |
| " | 17/4 | | Company resting. 1. O.R. Killed by shell. | M. |
| " | 18/4 | | Whole of Company moved by road to neighbourhood of ABEELE. Two Sections employed at night on making tracks between forward Bde H.Q. and Res. Bde. H.Q. at MONT NOIR. | M. |
| | | | INTERPRETER Mons HENRI LORENZ died from heart failure. | |
| ABEELE | 18/4 | | Company employed :- Individual training and games and Kit Inspection | M. |
| " | 19/4 | | Company employed :- do Jr. 18th | M. |
| " | 20/4 | | Company employed :- do do 19th | M. |
| " | 21/4 | | Capt E.F. KNIGHT M.C., R.E.S.R. joins Company and assumes Command of Company. Company moves to U. 12 b. 5. 5. near HONDEGHEM. Transport by road. Dismounted echelon by Buses. | M. |
| Mt HONDEGHEM | 22/4 | | O.C. Action Officer & senior N.C.Os went round works on 2nd Zone Defences. | NR |
| | 23/4 | | 4 Sections clearing hedges on 2nd Zone Defences. | NR |
| | 24/4 | | 3 Sections clearing hedges. 1 Section preparing mining Dumps. | NR |
| | 26/4 | | 3 Sections clearing hedges. 1 Section preparing mining Dumps. | NR |
| | 26/4 | | 1 Section mining. | NR |

Army Form C. 2118

# WAR DIARY
## INTELLIGENCE SUMMARY
(Erase heading not required.)

| Place | Date | Hour | Summary of Events and Information | Remarks and references to Appendices |
|---|---|---|---|---|
| Mt. HONDEGHEM. | 28/4 | | Company (10 mounted duties) moved by road to AU SOUVERAIN D. Sh. C.9.I. Transport moved by road to D.4. b. 1.9. 1 Section took over Demolitions of Bridge etc. 2 Sections working on 2nd phase posn. | JMR |
| AU SOUVERAIN | 29/4 | | 2 Sections worked on Strong Pts at PETIT SEC BOIS. 'Reserve Line. 1 Section on Tracks. 1 Section on Demolitions. | JMR |
| | 29/4 & 30/4 | | Work on Strong Pt. at PETIT SEC BOIS handed over to 455" (W.R.) Fd. Co. R.E. 1 Section in Reserve Line Wiring / Strong Pts. 1 Section on Tracks Wiring / Section and Demolitions. | JMR |

J.M.Wright.

30/4

MAJOR, R.E.
O.C. 497TH (KENT) FIELD CO: R.E.

C O N F I D E N T I A L

W A R   D I A R Y.

of

497TH (KENT) FIELD COY R.E

From 1/5/18 to 31/5/18

VOLUME No. 32.

39/228

Vol 27

# WAR DIARY
## or
## INTELLIGENCE SUMMARY.
*(Erase heading not required.)*

Army Form C. 2118.

| Place | Date | Hour | Summary of Events and Information | Remarks and references to Appendices |
|---|---|---|---|---|
| | 1918 | | | |
| Au SOONERAIN | 1/5 | | Company employed:- 2 Sections Reserve Line - 1 Section Tracks - 1 Section Demolitions | |
| " | 2/5 | | " - 1 Section erecting fresh Bridge remainder as for the 1st | |
| " | 3/5 | | " - do for 1st | |
| " | 4/5 | | " - 2 Sections Corps Bullet & Reserve Line - 2 Sections Demolitions + Tracks | |
| " | 5/5 | | Company (Dismounted Section) Riding, Drill Physical Exercises + Games | |
| " | 6/5 | | Company Employed:- 1 Section wiring & clearing at PTE MARQUETTE - 1 Section on Reserve Line - 2 Sections Tracks and Demolitions | |
| " | 7/5 | | " - 2 Sections constructing Reserve Line - 2 Sections Tracks, Demolitions & Rifles | |
| " | 8/5 | | " - do - for 7th | |
| " | 9/5 | | " - do - for 8th | |
| " | 10/5 | | " - do - for 9th | |
| " | 11/5 | | " - do - for 10th Left side of Reserve Line handed over to M55th Field Coy RE | |
| " | 12/5 | | " - do - for 11th Length to CLINEY from R XV Corps Officers taken over | |
| " | 13/5 | | " - 1 Section on Reserve Line - 1 Section Demolitions and Road Repairs - 2 Sections Inspection, Rifle Manual, Baths + Games | |
| " | 14/5 | | " - 2 Sections on Reserve Line, Tracks, Demolitions, 2 Sections Inspections, Drill, Baths + Games | |

# WAR DIARY or INTELLIGENCE SUMMARY.

Army Form C. 2118.

| Place | Date | Hour | Summary of Events and Information | Remarks and references to Appendices |
|---|---|---|---|---|
| AU SOUVERAIN | 15/5 | | Company Employed - 2 Sections on Reserve Line, 1 Section Sacks, Demolitions dugs Switch Line | |
| " | 16/5 | | do do 15th | |
| | | | 30 Other ranks (Reinforcements) joined Company from R.E. Base Depot | |
| " | 17/5 | | do do 16th | |
| " | 18/5 | | do do 14th | |
| " | 19/5 | | 1 Section on Reserve Line, 1 Section Sacks and Shelters for R.F.A. | |
| | | | 2 Sections Inspection, Rifle Manuel, Baths + Games | |
| " | 20/5 | | 2 Sections Inspection, Drill, Baths + Games | |
| | | | 1 Section on Reserve Line, 1 Section Shelters for R.F.A. Demolitions | |
| | | | Lieut. F.D. CLIFFE returns to duty from VI Corps Officers School | |
| " | 21/5 | | 2 Sections on LA MOTTE Switch Line, 1 Section in Sacks and R.F.A. Shelters | |
| | | | 1 Section Demolitions + Workshop | |
| " | 22/5 | | do do 21st | |
| " | 23/5 | | do do 22nd and Erection of Nis. Pat. | |
| " | 24/5 | | do do 23rd | |
| " | 25/5 | | 1 Section on LA MOTTE SWITCH, 1 Section on Shelters for R.F.A. 2 Sections Resting | |

# WAR DIARY
## or
## INTELLIGENCE SUMMARY

Army Form C. 2118.

| Place | Date | Hour | Summary of Events and Information | Remarks and references to Appendices |
|---|---|---|---|---|
| AU SOUVERAIN | 26/5 | | Company Employed:- 2 Sections on LA MOETE SWITCH, 1 Section Shelters for R.F.A. + 1 Section on Dug Outs | MC |
| " | 27/5 | | " " " do do 26th | |
| " | 28/5 | | " " " do do 27th | |
| " | 29/5 | | " " " do do 28th | |
| " | 30/5 | | " " " do do 29th | |
| " | 31/5 | | " " " do do 30th | |
| | | | Effective Strength of Company Officers 4 Dismounted O.R. 152 Dismounts O.R. 50 | |

M King M[?]

MAJOR, R.E.
O.O. 497TH (KENT) FIELD CO: R.E.

CONFIDENTIAL

WAR DIARY.

of

497TH (KENT) FIELD Co., R.E.

From 1-6-18 to 30-6-18

VOLUME No. 33

Army Form C. 2118.

# WAR DIARY
## or
## INTELLIGENCE SUMMARY.
*(Erase heading not required.)*

Instructions regarding War Diaries and Intelligence Summaries are contained in F. S. Regs., Part II. and the Staff Manual respectively. Title pages will be prepared in manuscript.

| Place | Date | Hour | Summary of Events and Information | Remarks and references to Appendices |
|---|---|---|---|---|
| | 1918 | | | |
| Dismounted portion of Coy | 1/6 to 6/6 | | 2 Sections on LA MOTTE SWITCH LINE. 2 Sections on Shelters for R.E.A. Roads. Tracks & Demolitions. 1 Section training, bathing every other day. | |
| Au SOUVERAIN Mounted portion of Company D.T.C.I.C.9 | 7/6 to 14/6 | | 2 Section LA MOTTE SWITCH LINE. 1 Section R.E.A. Shelters Tracks Roads Railway. Au SOUVERAIN to LA MOTTE and Demolitions. 1 Section training | |
| " | 15/6 | | So far 15 ½ Lieut. D. GILLESPIE leave to U.K. 14 days | |
| " | 16/6 | | So far 15 ½ Lieut. B.S. ALLEN to Gas Officers Model | |
| " | 17/6 | | | 9/11R |
| " | 18/6 & 19/6 | | 2 Sections LA MOTTE SWITCH LINE. 2 Section R.E.A. Shelters Roads Railway. Au SOUVERAIN to LA MOTTE and Demolitions | |
| " | 20/6 | | 2 Sections Bathing & loading transport. 1 Section LA MOTTE SWITCH LINE 1 Section Iron Walker tracks. Dismounted portion of Coy. handed over hulks to 223rd Field Co R.E. moves to H.55 at Field Coys Billets at 3.69/D.9.b.53 | |
| " | 21/6 | | Handing over work to 210 st Field 600 R.E. Company moves to EEK HOUT CASTEEL C.69.15 | |
| EEK HOUT CASTEEL C.69.c.1.5. | 22/6 | | Taking over the EAST HAZEBROUCK DEFENCES from 223rd Field Coy of R.E. and making camp | |
| " | 23/6 to 24/6 | | 3 Sections on E. HAZEBROUCK DEFENCES. 1 Section training | |

# WAR DIARY
## or
## INTELLIGENCE SUMMARY

Army Form C. 2118.

| Place | Date | Hour | Summary of Events and Information | Remarks and references to Appendices |
|---|---|---|---|---|
| EEKHOUT (ASTEEL) | 25/6 | | Report before 24th. Capt G.E. LINES proceeded to Corps Officers' School. | [9/13] |
| | 26/6 | | Do for 25th. I think B.S. ALLAN rejoined Coy from Corps Officers' School. | |
| | 28/6 | | Do for 26th. | |
| | 29/6 | | | |
| | | | Effective strength of Company. 7 Officers 153 Dismounted O.R. 53 mounted O.R. | |

[Signature]

MAJOR, R.E.
O.C. 497TH (KENT) FIELD CO. R.E.

Vol 29

CONFIDENTIAL

WAR DIARY.

of

497TH (KENT) FIELD CO., R.E.

FROM 1-7-18 TO 31-7-18

VOLUME No. 34.

Army Form C. 2118.

# WAR DIARY
## or
## INTELLIGENCE SUMMARY.
(Erase heading not required.)

| Place | Date | Hour | Summary of Events and Information | Remarks and references to Appendices |
|---|---|---|---|---|
| EEK HOUT CASTEEL (C.6.c.15.) | 1-7-18 | | 3 Sections on E. HAZEBROUCK DEFENCES. 1 Section Training. | |
| | 2-7-18 | | do. for 1st. Lieut. D. GILLESPIE rejoined coy. from leave to U.K. | |
| | 3-7-18 | | do. for 1st. Capt. G.E. LINES rejoined coy. from XV.Corps Officers School | |
| | 4-7-18 to 14-7-18 | | 3 Sections on E. HAZEBROUCK DEFENCES and 1 Section Training | |
| | 15-7-18 | | 3 Sections on E. HAZEBROUCK DEFENCES. 1 Section Wounded Sick escort to BANDRINGHEM by motor lorries from HAZEBROUCK | |
| BANDRINGHEM (F.18.C.1.5) | 16-7-18 | | Inspections and Cleaning up. Lieut. F.D. CLEVELY leave to U.K. | |
| | 17-7-18 to 19-7-18 | | Training | |
| | 20-7-18 | | Inspection of Company by O.C. R.E. 29th Division | |
| | 21-7-18 | | Church Parade. | |
| | 22-7-18 | | Coy. moves by march route to BAVINCHOVE | |
| | 23-7-18 | | Training | |
| BAVINCHOVE (Cite a.6.5) | 24-7-18 | | Training | |
| | 30-7-18 | | Training. Lieut. D. GILLESPIE admitted Hospital | |
| | 31-7-18 | | Training | |
| | | | Effective Strength of Coy. 7 Officers 202 other ranks | |

MAJOR R.E.
O.C. 497TH (KENT) FIELD CO: R.E.

CONFIDENTIAL

WAR DIARY.

of

497th Field Coy RE (T)

From 1/8/18. to 31/8/18.

VOLUME No. 35

# WAR DIARY
## or
## INTELLIGENCE SUMMARY.
*(Erase heading not required.)*

Army Form C. 2118.

| Place | Date | Hour | Summary of Events and Information | Remarks and references to Appendices |
|---|---|---|---|---|
| BAVIN'CHOVE C.16.a.b.5 | 1/8/18 | | Baths & Training. Taking over work from 2nd Australian Tunl Coy. R.E. | |
| | 2/8/18 | | LIEUT. F.D. CLEVELY rejoined from leave | |
| | 3 - 4 8/18 | | Dismounted Sections move by march route to 27/W.13.c.55 Taking Section in 27/W.15.d.9.9 | |
| 27/W.13.b.55 | 5.8.18 | | Work on own Support line. 9 reconnoitring CAPT. G.E. HINES leave to U.K. | |
| | | | Work on own Support line. Demolitions & accommodation for 2 Sections at W.23 b.4. Taking over ¾ line from London Irish to R.E. and landing over own Support line | |
| | 6-8- 6/18 | | 2 Sections work on ¾ lane. 2 Sections Support line. Demolitions & accommodation | |
| | 9.8.18 | | 2 Sections on ¾ lane. 2 Sections on Support line. Demolitions. 2 Sections over Sulter & W.23.a.b.4 | |
| | 10-13 8/18 | | 2 Sections on ¾ lane. 2 Sections on Support line & dug-outs | |
| | 14.8.18 15.16 8/18 | | Baths & medical inspection. Demolitions. New Support line. LIEUT. A.D. McKEISH M.G. wounded | |
| | 17/8/18 | | 2 Sections on ¾ lane. 3 Sections on Support line. Tracks, Demolitions and roads | |
| | | | 2 Sections ¾ lane. 3 Sections tracks. Demolitions Roads & making advance dumps. Survey of bridges over METEREN BECQUE completed, also tracks marked out | |
| | 18.8.18 | | Observation reports with 87th Infantry Brigade. Capture of OUTERSTEENE RIDGE. Run made and wiring material | |
| | 19.8.18 | | 3 Sections assisting the METEREN BECQUE forming dumps for making trench tracks | |

# WAR DIARY or INTELLIGENCE SUMMARY

Army Form C. 2118.

| Place | Date | Hour | Summary of Events and Information | Remarks and references to Appendices |
|---|---|---|---|---|
| 27/W.13 & 23 | 19.8.18 | | (continued) Rifts and damaged roads. 1 Section to 7. Kons. S.A.A. C.E. LINES | |
| | 20.21 8/18 | | organised fatigue from train. 1 Section 7. Kons. 2 Sections Repairing Roads. Making Fundingtracks 7. Bridge etc | |
| | 22.8.18 | | METEREN BECQUE Demolition. LIEUT D. GILLESPIE arrived 20.8.15. 2 Sections reconnoitring and laying out New Support Line. Repairing roads 7. Bridges. Demolitions. 2 Sections 7. Kons | |
| | 23.8.18 | | H.Q. & 2 Sections moved to W.23.a.6.4. 2nd Section moved to 27/W.24.c.9.6. 2 Sections with 7. Kons. 1 Section reconnoitring bridges & demolitions. 1 Section making of approaches to for day &N.G. | |
| RATTE HILL 27/N.22.a.6.4 | 24.8.18 | | 2 Sections with 7. Kons. 1 Section reconnaissance of bridges & Demolitions. 1 Section reconnaissance & design for Coy H.Q. and pulling up rail/wg on Right. B.G. I.H.Q. 1 Section | |
| | 25.8.18 | | 2 Sections Baths & Laundries. 1 Section 7. Kons. 1 Section M.O. II. LIEUT K.S. TOMSON joined Coy. | |
| | 26.8.18 | | 1 Section Baths & laundries. 3 Sections with 7. Kons. Demolition Right & Left | |
| | 27.7.18 28.8.18 | | Rd Mn. M.D. Making two new bridge. Improving approaches to bridge over METEREN BECQUE. 2 Sections 7. Kons. 2 Sections Right & Left B.Gs. D.G. & Bridges Demolitions & roads. | |
| | | | LIEUT G.M. ELLIOTT Leave to U.K. 28.8.18 | |

Army Form C. 2118.

# WAR DIARY
## or
## INTELLIGENCE SUMMARY.
*(Erase heading not required.)*

Instructions regarding War Diaries and Intelligence Summaries are contained in F. S. Regs., Part II. and the Staff Manual respectively. Title pages will be prepared in manuscript.

| Place | Date | Hour | Summary of Events and Information | Remarks and references to Appendices |
|---|---|---|---|---|
| KLITE HILL 27/V.23.a.b.4. | 30.8.18 | | 2 Sections BRAHMIN BRIDGE and BRIDGE MAINTENANCE | |
| | 31.8.18 | | 2 Sections BRAHMIN BRIDGE. 2 Section on forward roads Ytardying 36ᵗʰ/F.4.6.7.4 centre | A.R. |
| | | | Mounted Section moved from 27/V.15.d.9.9 to KLITE HILL (27/w.23.a.b.4) | |
| | | | Effective Strength of Company 7 Officers 204 other ranks | |

D.W.
MAJOR, R.E.
O.C. 497ᵀᴴ (KENT) FIELD CO. R.E.

Vol 31

CONFIDENTIAL

WAR DIARY.

of

497th Field Coy R.E.

From 1/9/18 to 30/9/18

VOLUME No. XXXVI.

Army Form C. 2118.

# WAR DIARY
## or
## INTELLIGENCE SUMMARY.
(Erase heading not required.)

Instructions regarding War Diaries and Intelligence Summaries are contained in F. S. Regs., Part II. and the Staff Manual respectively. Title pages will be prepared in manuscript.

| Place | Date | Hour | Summary of Events and Information | Remarks and references to Appendices |
|---|---|---|---|---|
| WHITE HILL 27/W.22.b.64 | 1/9/18 | | 2 Sections work on road GAPA CROSS ROADS (27/X.22.a.2.1) to VERITY CROSSING. 1 Section (364/F.5.c.2.6.) working bridge over water at 364/F.4.d.7.2. 1 Section on BRAHMIN BRIDGE. (27/X.20.c.8.6) | |
| X.21.d.5.8. | 2/9/18 | 6.04 | Wo. transport move to X.21.a.5.8. 2 Sections work on road GAPA CROSS ROADS (27/X.22.a.2.1) to VERITY CROSSING (36/A.F.c.2.6) 1 Section on Water Supply Lynn Square 36/A.2.c.9.d. 1 Section on [trestle aple line] bridge at 36/A.2.c.95.00. Company moves to A.2.d.5.8. | |
| A.2.d.5.8. | 3/9/18 | | 1 Section on Water Supply on Sqn 36/A.2.c.9.d. 1 Section on tin trestle load bridge at H.4.c.7.6 36/A.2.c.95.00. 1 Section on road 36/A.3.a.2.4.6. 1 Section moves to A.6.d.4.6 and work on main ARMENTIERES - BAILLEUL RD | |
| | 4/9/18 | | 1 Section Water Supply LA CRECHE. 1 Section on lookout B.8.a.7.7. 1 Section bridging (tin trestle bridge) at culvert Km 3 at B.2.c.0.3. 3 Sections move to A.6.d.4.6 | |
| A.6.d.4.6. | 5/9/18 | | 1 Section Water Supply LA CRECHE. 1 Section on tin trestle load bridge B.2.c.0.3. 1 Section on road LA CRECHE. 1 Section making way round [bridge] crater at Railway crossing 36/H.6.c.6.7. | |
| | 6/9/18 | | 1 Section Water Supply BAILLEUL - ARMENTIERES ROAD. 1 Section making [way round] crater at T.29.d.3.5 and T.30.c.45.70. 1 Section on BAILLEUL - ARMENTIERES way round crater at | |

# WAR DIARY
## or
## INTELLIGENCE SUMMARY.

Army Form C. 2118.

| Place | Date | Hour | Summary of Events and Information | Remarks and references to Appendices |
|---|---|---|---|---|
| Aladdib | 6/9/18 | | R.O.A.D. 1 Section in Reserve | |
| | 7/9/18 | | 1 Section on Water Supply BAILLEUL-ARMENTIERES ROAD. 2 Sections on BAILLEUL - ARMENTIERES ROAD. 1 Section in Reserve. | |
| | 8/9/18 | | 1 Section Water Supply PONT D'ACHELLES. 1 Section preparing material for road round crater at 36T.29.d.3.5. and 36T.30.c.4.5.70. 1 Section BAILLEUL ARMENTIERES ROAD. Salving & Repairing Road Sweeper | |
| | 9/9/18 | | 1 Section preparing material for road round crater at 36T.29.d.3.5. and 36T.30.c.4.5.70. 2 Sections on roads in squares B.19.C.H.I.R.27.telephone poles 27/X.19.a.0.6 | MK MF |
| 2/X.19.a.c.6 | 10/9/18 | | Lieut R.C. GILLESPIE attached H.Q. R.E. 29th Division. | |
| | 11/9/18 | | Coy move by road to HAZEBROUCK. Billeted at Second Army Workshops 27/V.22.c.30.25 | |
| HAZEBROUCK | 12/9/18 and 13 and 14/9/18 | | Transport lines V.21.b.7.2. Kit Inspection & Repairing billets. Lieut G.M. ELLIOT rejoined coy from leave | |
| | 15/9/18 16 and 17/9/18 | | Drawing Church Parade Training | |

Army Form C. 2118.

# WAR DIARY
## or
## INTELLIGENCE SUMMARY.
*(Erase heading not required.)*

Instructions regarding War Diaries and Intelligence Summaries are contained in F. S. Regs., Part II. and the Staff Manual respectively. Title pages will be prepared in manuscript.

| Place | Date | Hour | Summary of Events and Information | Remarks and references to Appendices |
|---|---|---|---|---|
| HAZEBROUCK | 18/9/18 | | Boy sent to 28/H.30.d.06. Dismantled portion of Boy by lorries. Mounted portion and cycled by road. | |
| 28/H.30.d.06 | 19/9/18 | | Lt. D. GILLESPIE joined Boy from H.Q.R.E. | |
| H.30.C.7.1. | 20/9/18 22/9/18 | | Work on Russian H.Q. BRAKE CAMP. Boy moved in billets at 28/H.30.C.7.1. | |
| | 23/9/18 | | Work on Russian H.Q. BRAKE CAMP. | |
| | | | 3 Sections work on Russian H.Q. BRAKE CAMP. 1 Section, less transport, moved to Infantry Barracks YPRES. | |
| | 24/9/18 | | 3 Sections work on Russian H.Q. BRAKE CAMP. 1 Section repairing dug outs Infantry Barracks, YPRES. | |
| | 25/9/18 26/9/18 | | 3 Sections work on Russian H.Q. BRAKE CAMP. 1 Section repairing dug outs Infantry Barracks, YPRES. 1 Section Barracks YPRES and constructing foot bridge at I.8.d.12. | |
| | 27/9/18 | | 3 Sections less transport moved forward to Infantry Barracks, YPRES. Section repairing Infantry Barracks, YPRES and rebuilding bridge at I.8.d.12. | |
| INFANTRY BARRACKS, YPRES | 28/9/18 | | Operations See Operation Order No 2 attached. Capture of high ground East of YPRES. Main Road opened up to HOOGE. Sunken duckboard bridge wired at I.18.a.2.7. Mule track opened up to GLENCORSE WOOD. Casualties - 1 O.R. Killed, 1 O.R. Wounded. | |
| | 29/9/18 | | Company moved forward to HOOGE 28/J.13.a.1.9. Boy work on CHATEAU WOOD ROAD. | |

Army Form C. 2118.

# WAR DIARY
## or
## INTELLIGENCE SUMMARY.
*(Erase heading not required.)*

Instructions regarding War Diaries and Intelligence Summaries are contained in F. S. Regs., Part II. and the Staff Manual respectively. Title pages will be prepared in manuscript.

| Place | Date | Hour | Summary of Events and Information | Remarks and references to Appendices |
|---|---|---|---|---|
| INFANTRY BARRACKS YPRES | 29/9/18 | | and men MENIN ROAD in Squares J.13.d and J.14.c. | } AAR |
| HOOGE | 30/9/18 | | Dismounted Sections move to GLENCORSE WOOD J.14.a.3.6. North on CHATEAU WOOD | |
| | | | Road and men MENIN ROAD in Squares J.13.d and J.14.c. | |

M. K...
Major R.E.,
O.C. 497th (Kent) Field Co., R.E.

497th (Kent) Field Co., R.E.    SECRET.
Operation Order No. 2.

Ref. Sheets 28 N.W. and
28 N.E. 1/20,000.

1./ Reference. (a) C.R.E. 29th Division O.O. No. 76.
(b) Scheme for Roads, Tracks & Tramways
C.R.E.'s 65/3.
(c) Communications
29th Division Operation Instruction No. 3.
(d) Medical Arrangements.
A.D.M.S., 29th Division No. S.R. 11/194

2./ On a date ("J" Day) and at a hour to be notified later the 29th Division is attacking with a view to the capture of the high ground EAST OF YPRES.

The 87th Brigade on the right and the 86th Brigade on the left on a frontage of some 1,600 yards from ZILLEBEKE to the YPRES - MENIN ROAD.

3./ The work of the R.E. and Pioneers will be to open up.
(a) roads for the Gunners
As the infantry will advance so quickly the F.A. will be out of range after the 1st objective is taken and so will have to move up at Zero plus 2¼ hours as follows.

One Brigade R.F.A. by batteries in succession into action in the neighbourhood of RIFLE FARM.

One Brigade R.F.A. by batteries in succession by MENIN ROAD into action about the ZILLEBEKE - RAILWAY WOOD ROAD.

15th Brigade R.H.A. will be held in readiness to advance at an hour's notice.
(b) Mule Tracks "A" and B

4./ The attached tracing shews roads, which will be.-
(1) (a) opened up before Zero.
(b) started on as soon after Zero as possible
(c) worked on as soon as those in (b) are finished.
(2) The mule tracks "A" and "B".
The units responsible for the work are also given.

5./ Labour detailed to work with this Company.
  (a) "B" Company of 1/2nd Monmouth Pioneers
      billetted MAGAZINE, YPRES.
  (b) 2 Officers and 60 T.M.B. INFANTRY BARRACKS, YPRES.

6./ Work to be done by this Company.
  (a) Open up MENIN ROAD from FRONT LINE to
      BIRR CROSS ROADS I.17.b.25.80. thence to I.17.c.7.6.
      and I.11.d.4.3. for Field Artillery.

Labour under Lieut Elliott
      No. 4 Section, 497th (Kent) Field Co., R.E.
      2 Platoons "B" Coy. 1/2nd Monmouth Pioneers
      60 T.M.B.

      From aeroplane photos the worst piece looks
to be from BIRR CROSS ROADS. I.17.b.25.80. to I.17.b.2.5.
so labour will have to be concentrated on this. As soon
as one piece is finished or handed over the men must
be leap frogged forward. No tiddivating will be
done, simply one way road made.

Notice Boards. Lieut Elliott will be responsible that
the following notice boards are erected. —
      LEINSTER FARM
      I.17.a.8.3.
      BIRR CROSS ROADS
      I.17.b.7.8.
      LEINSTER ROAD (3)

Transport. 5 G.S. Limbers from the 1/2nd Monmouth
      Pioneers. For details see appendix A.

Material    50 tons of road metal  ⎫ at I.10.c.9.5.
            100 7" Pit Props.       ⎭
            3 Artillery Bridges at School Dump I.9.d.3.1.
            Planking may be taken up from
            LEINSTER ROAD South of I.17.c.7.5.
            20 wheelbarrows  ⎫
            Sandbags         ⎬ will be brought up
            Spikes           ⎭ by the G.S. Limbers

            The Corps will be working up the YPRES.
MENIN ROAD and if they catch us up the work
should be handed over and our parties pushed on

3.

forward. Also if the 510th Field Co, R.E. finish their other jobs in time, they will take over this work and our party less T.M.B will move forward to assist No. 1 and 3 Sections

If work is finished early enough all labour will be switched on to the plank road by HOOGE under Lieut Gillespie.

A R.F.A. liason officer has been detailed to reconnoitre roads, and keep in touch with his H.Q. so that they may know when the road is open. All assistance should be given to this officer

The Gunners will have an advance report centre at I.9.a.65.60.

(a) First construct mule track "B" from BIRR CROSS ROADS I.17.b.25.80. to HOOGE, this will mean making a way by the culvert at I.18.a.2.7. next convert same into road for F.A.

Erecting trestle Bridge over gap at Culvert I.18.a.2.7. The gap at Culvert from Aeroplane photos looks to be about 35' so two trestles will be necessary. As soon as this is completed the labour will be switched either on to work in (a) or (c) depending on the state of completion of (a).

Notice Boards. Sergt Luxford will be responsible for the erection of the following notice boards.
10 – TRACK B
THE CULVERT.
HOOGE.

Labour. No. 2 Section 497th (Kent) Field Co R.E.

Transport Two trestle wagons will bring up the trestles under arrangements made by Capt Lines. If any of the equipment is damaged a wire will be immediately dispatched to the C.R.E.

(c.) Construct Mule Track "B" from HOOGE to GLENCORSE WOOD when laying this track out it must be taken into consideration that a road for F.A. will be made later

4.

Labour. Under Lieut. D Gillespie R.E.
Nos 1 and 3 Sections, 497th (Kent) Field Co. R.E.
2 Platoons Pioneers

Notice Boards. Lieut. Gillespie will be responsible
that the following are erected.
CHATEAU WOOD ROAD
at I.18.a.9.6. and J.7.d.9.2.
JAROON CROSS ROADS.
at J.7.d.9.2.
PLUMBERS DRIVE
at J.13.b.5.0. and J.14.a.5.5.
GLENCORSE WOOD
J.14.a.9.6.
TRACK "B" 140.

Transport. Pack Animals. Details to be arranged by
Capt. Lines. See Appendix "A"

(d) As there is not very much work required to make Track "B"
labour will be put on immediately to convert it into one
way road for F.A.

Labour. All labour as it becomes available will be
put on. This will be organised in gangs as follows:-
(I) Clearing Gang.
Pull up and clear on to one side all
planks that are damaged.
(II). Formation Gang.
Make up the formations ready for laying.
(III) Laying Gang.
Lay stringers and chessing ready for spiking.
(IV) Fixing Gang.
Spike down.
(V) Scrounging Gang.
Collect material (from Southern direction)
and dump on site.

Material. Slabbing, spikes etc will be delivered at
HOOGE under arrangements by C.O. 1/2nd Monmouth
Pioneers. Lieut Gillespie will see that a party

is detailed to unload all wagons as far up as they can get as soon as they arrive.

There are 6 Artillery Bridges at SCHOOL DUMP I.9.d.3.1. which may be used for this road. Lieut. Gillespie may use the trestle wagons that bring up the trestles for transporting these bridges.

7./ <u>Transport.</u> Details as appendix "A."

8./ <u>Tools.</u> Section Officers will prepare a list of all tools required, stating how these will be carried forward.

Tool Cart equipment will not be touched but kept absolutely ready for any move.

Each man will carry 10 sandbags. N.C.O's and a proportion of sappers & drivers will take wire cutters.

There are a number of buckets available which will be used for emptying the water from shell holes; the holes will then be filled with sandbags of dry earth.

9./ <u>B. Teams</u> O's. C. No's 2 and 3 Sections will not go forward with their sections.

One senior and one junior N.C.O. and 3 Sappers per section will be left behind.

O.C. Sections will submit at once to Coy. Office the working strength of their Section after deducting above.

10./ <u>Reconnoitring.</u> Section Officers will make sure that they have sufficient guides who have reconnoitred the ground to take their men forward on "J" day.

Lieut. Clively will reconnoitre "B" Track with a view of making a one way F.A. road giving in his report the state of road, labour & time required to repair, and stores required. Maps have been specially issued on which these reports will be made out and sent back.

6.

Copies of report will be sent
(a) H.Q. R.E. GOLDFISH CHATEAU.
(b) ~~Copy to~~ π LT. K.S. JEWSON.

O's.C. No's 1 and 4 Sections will reconnoitre the neighbourhood of their jobs for material, and report to ~~him also~~ π LT. JEWSON anything of importance

11./ <u>Telephone and Telegraph</u>.

Main Route.

GOLDFISH CHATEAU
MACHINE GUN FARM
RAMPARTS
I.11.a.5.8. and I.15.c.5.7.
} Messages may be sent from any of these stations.

thence in a general direction along MENIN ROAD.

Visual Stations.

Main St. I.16.b.5.8
also (a) I.16.b.0.4.
(b) I.17.c.6.8.
(c) J.14.c.1.7.

12./ <u>Locations "J" Day</u>

R.E. H.Q. GOLDFISH CHATEAU. H.11.c.9.6.

86TH BDE.
87TH "
88TH "
} RAMPARTS, YPRES. I.14.b.2.9

455TH FIELD Co, R.E., LILLE GATE. I.14.a.95.25.

510TH FIELD Co, R.E. MACHINE GUN SIDING H.12.a.6.4.

At Zero. O.C., 497th (Kent) Field Co, R.E. 86th BDE. RAMPARTS, YPRES.

π Lieut K.S. JEWSON    DO    DO    DO.

No's. 1, 2 and 3 Sections, 497th Field Co. R.E.
    INFANTRY BARRACKS, YPRES.

2 Platoons. 1/2nd Monmouth Pioneers. MAGAZINE, YPRES.

No. 4 Section, 497th (Kent) Field Co. R.E.
2 Platoons 1/2nd Monmouth Pioneers
T.M.B.
} To be notified later.

CAPT. LINES R.E., MACHINE GUN SIDING.

13./ <u>Moving ~~forward~~</u>. Orders for moving forward will be sent by runner from O.C. 497th (Kent) Field Co. R.E.

7.

For this purpose O's.C. Nos 1, 2 and 4 Sections will each detail two runners to report to the O.C. on "I." evening. These runners must know the way from Brigade H.Q. RAMPARTS to the Section positions at Zero.

Nos. 1 and 2 Section runners will be from the "B" team. No. 4 Section runner will proceed with his Section.

O.C. Sections will acknowledge their orders by phone if possible otherwise by runner.

14./ <u>Report Kentre</u>. Lieut. K.S. JEWSON will be at Bde H.Q. RAMPARTS at Zero to receive any messages until Zero + 4 hours, then move forward to I 16.a.5.8.

Section Officers will report progress, handing over, completion of jobs etc to Lieut JEWSON who will keep H.Q.R.E. informed.

15./ <u>Dumps</u>. The C.R.E. will form a dump of slabs, nails and spikes at HELL FIRE CORNER, under the R.S.M. as soon after Zero as possible. All available wagons will take slabs forward to HOOGE from this dump.

16./ <u>Dress</u>. Fighting Order and "I" days rations

17./ <u>Packsets</u>. All kits will be left packed under guard of "B" team at INFANTRY BARRACKS.

"B" Team must be ready to load up & move camp if it is necessary for the Company to get nearer their work.

Capt. Lines will arrange that transport is detailed for this move.

O's.C. Nos 1 and 4 Sections will look out for suitable places for a camp. A certain number of bivouac sheets are being issued.

MAJOR, R.E.
O.C. 497TH (KENT) FIELD CO. R.E.

SECRET    Appendix Ⓐ    Copy No. 9

Operation Order No. 3
by
497th (Kent) Field Coy. R.E.    13-10-18

Map Ref. Sheets
28 + 29 1/40,000

(1) At zero i.e. "H" hour on "J" day, the II Corps is attacking on the front between VIJFWEGEN on the Right, & point F.25.6.8.5 on the left, the 1st objective of the Corps being the HEULE – INGLEMUNSTER Railway.

(2) The 29th Division will attack between the 36th Division on its right & the 9th Division on its left.

(3) The attack will be carried out by the 88th Brigade on the right, & the 86th Brigade on the left up to the line marked 1st Objective on Map "A" attached.
The 87th Brigade will be in Divisional Reserve.

(4) The attack for a depth of 3500 yards will be carried out under cover of a creeping barrage. There will be no preliminary bombardment. After cessation of the creeping barrage the advance will be covered by heavy artillery.
After firing the creeping barrage, the Divisional Artillery will commence advancing at about zero plus 1¾ hours, in support of the attacking Infantry Brigades.

(5) Employment of 497th Field Coy. R.E.
(a) The 13th Battery of the 17th Bde. R.F.A. will go forward with the 88th Inf. Bde. & 1 Section R.E. will assist this battery forward.
(b) Reconnoitring the roads in the 88th Bde. area & doing any R.E. work other than purely road repairs that may crop up. In particular bridging the HEULEBECK at L.15.b.1.9 & L.8.d.5.5 if existing bridges have been destroyed ~~for~~ for Field Artillery & ~~for Heavy Artillery~~.
(c) Erecting notice boards.
(d) Exploit drinking water supply in the 88th Inf. Bde. area.

(6) Distribution of Work
(a) No. 3 Section will assist the 13th Battery forward & will assemble less, Tool cart, forage cart & cycles at

2

the Battery position ~~at H~~ at H-1 hour.

O.C. No. 3 Section with 2 runners will reconnoitre the forward route, for the Battery with Lieut. MEESON R.F.A. as early as possible. The proposed route will be K.17.c.0.8 – K.17.d.0.4 – K.18.c.0.5 – K.18.b.0.2 – K.18.b.3.1 – L.13.a.4.8 – L.14.b.5.2 – L.9.c.8.0.

As soon as the situation permits the section will go forward along above route doing any work necessary & meet Lieut JEWSON at ALGITHA FM. K.18.b.1.1.

The 13th Battery R.F.A. are arranging to take forward two German Artillery Bridges on wheels. (12' long overall, 7' roadway)

No. 3 Section will keep with 13th Battery until another Battery leap-frogs, in which case the section will move forward with the foremost battery. O.C. No. 3 Section will keep the O.C. informed of his movements.

Separate arrangements are being made for dealing with GWEN'S BRIDGE L.15.c.1.9. as early as possible.

TOOLS Each sapper will carry 10 sandbags, & a shovel, except one who will carry a 5ft. Xcut saw. One sapper in three will also carry large wirecutters.

In addition the following tools will be carried by 2 pack animals.

| | |
|---|---|
| 1 – 3ft. Xcut saw | 2 – Felling axes |
| 2 – hand saws | 2 Hand " |
| 1 – maul | 2 " hammers |
| 1 – Sledge hammer | nails 6", 4", 3" |
| 1 – Crowbar (short) | sandbags |
| 4 – prs. wirecutters | 2 – 2" lashings |
| 4 – Picks | |

Situation permitting No. 3 ~~Section~~ Toolcart will have moved forward to neighbourhood of GWEN'S BRIDGE by H+5.

No. 3 Section will camp on J/J+1 night near the Battery it is assisting & will report location to O.C. so that Section Transport can rejoin.

(b) (1) O.C. No. 4 Section with two runners from No. 1 Section will reconnoitre roads in the 88th Inf. Bde. Area, sending back by the two runners early information to O.C. at Bde. H.Q. L.1c.3.0. about GWEN BRIDGE

## 3

L 15.6.1.9 & ETHELS BRIDGE L.8.d.5.5
  O.C. No 4 Section will assemble at Bde. H.Q.
L.1.c.3.0. at H hour with O.C.

(2) If the above bridges are destroyed, O.C. No 1 Section will on receipt of orders from O.C. bring forward Nos 1 & 4 Sections, ~~together with~~ (less forage carts + officers rides) together with No 3 Section Tool Cart & the two trestle wagons each with a 30 ft bridge & bridge the gaps in the above order of priority. ~~for~~ for Field Artillery ~~afterwards of 10 ton~~ ~~and last~~. Roads permitting, section cyclists will proceed in advance to GWENS BRIDGE & commence work. ~~10 Ton Bridge will be at least of distance itself.~~

The F.A. Bridge, must be sited to one side of the road ~~so that the 10 Ton bridge can be erected without interfering with traffic~~.

Nos 1 & 4 Sections will camp near the site of the work until completion or handing over. ~~Material~~ O.C. No 1 Section will make early reconnaissance for heavy bridging material, so that as soon as trestle wagons are unloaded, they can be used for collecting same.

(c) O.C. No 2 Section will be responsible for erecting the following notice boards:=

| | |
|---|---|
| RICHMOND X ROADS | L.7.c.9.1. |
| DEDIZEELE HOEK. | L.14.b.1.5. |
| ETHELS BRIDGE | L.8.d.5.6 |
| AXHOLME X ROADS. | L.8.d.5.4. |
| GWEN'S BRIDGE | L.15.b.1.9. |
| PENNY CORNER. | L.16.d.6.6. |
| | L.17.a.1.8. |
| KOHINOOR X ROADS | L.17.a.5.9. |
| | L.11.b.9.3 |
| BAT CORNER. | L.17.b.7.9. |
| BARN FORK | L.12.c.8.3 |
| TILLEUL F.M. | G.13.b.4.3. |
| | G.15.a.3.5. |
| SALINES | G.15.b.4.7. |

4

HEULE        G.10.c.9.9.

       G.16.b.7.1

WINDMILL    .G.15.b.7.1
       G.11.c.5.5.

The notice board party will take brushes & paint so that other notices can be made.

(d) O.C. No 2 Section will also be responsible for the exploitation of drinking water supply in the 88th Inf. Bde. Area, forward of LEDEGHEM inclusive & will have the assistance of an R.A.M.C. N.C.O. & testing set.

Particular attention must be paid to the labelling of supplies. The R.A.M.C. N.C.O. will carry a supply of labels, & small boards giving map location will also be erected at these point.

Locations of good drinking water will be reported at the earliest possible opportunity to the C.R.E. & O.C.

Tools. Each man will carry 10 sandbags & a shovel or pick in the proportion of 5 shovels to 1 pick. (Nos 1, 2 & 4 Sections.)

(8) H.Q. & Transport. Two pontoon wagons with teams & drivers will be attached to 455th Field Coy R.E. from 15.30 on J-1 day & will take two days rations.

(7) ASSEMBLY Nos 1, 2, & 4 Sections less forage carts & officers riders will move off from K.8.a.2.2 at H+½ hour. & will proceed by the following route:— K.7.d.6.6.— K.14.a.5.8 — K.5.c.1.9. — K.11.b.9.4 — K.12.a.8.5 — K.12.b.5.1 — K.12.d.1.6. — RICHMOND X Roads L.7.c.9.1 — DADIZEELE HOEK, L.14.b.1.5. — L.8.d.5.4 — GWEN'S BRIDGE L.15.b.1.9.

At K.9.b.5.8 a halt will be made pending receipt of orders from O.C.

(8) H.Q. & TRANSPORT

One pontoon wagon with teams & drivers will be attached to 455th Field Coy. R.E. from 15.30 on J-1 day & will take two days rations and forage and 1 Bivouac sheet with them.

One extra trestle wagon with teams is being attached to the Coy. & will report at J.12.a.4.6. at 15.00 on J-1 day. This wagon will be loaded with 30' trestle bridge in addition to the Coy. wagon already similarly loaded.

All transport except that already detailed will be loaded & ready to move off by H+5 hours & will go forward under the C.S.M. on receipt of orders from O.C. In the event of Nos 1 & 4 Sections camping near GWEN'S BRIDGE L.15.b.1.9. O.C. No 1 Section will detail a guide who will be on the look out for C.S.M. & guide No 1 and No 4 Forage Carts to their Camp.

(9) GENERAL

(a) R.E. Dumps.

There are R.E. Dumps located at:- K.12.b.6.2 containing:- 20 Duckboards, 150' – 3"×2", 1000 sandbags, 20 shovels, 10 picks, 28 lb. 2" nails ½ cwt. 3" and 4" nails, 1 cwt. 6" nails

DADIZEELE K.12.a.2.9. :- 20 wheelbarrows
300 – 10' lengths 6"×6"
5000' run of 2"×1½"
4 – 22' RSJ 6"×5"
18 – 14' RSJ 3¼"×7"
4 crates, glass.

LEDEGHEM L.8.a. (It is proposed to
L.2.c. make this the Div. Dump.
L.1.C.30

(b) NOTICE BOARDS

All bridges will be notice boarded as to their load by the Section that construct

6

the bridge. All sections will take forward paint and brushes so that N.B's. can be made on site.

(c) <u>LOCATIONS</u>.

The O.C. will keep in touch with G.O.C. 88th Inf. Bde. & O.C. 17 Bde. R.F.A & at ZERO will be at L.1.c.3.0.

At "H" hour the H.Q. of formation will be as follows :-

D.H.Q.          K.7.c.4.8 ) will probably move to K.6.c.4.5
H.Q.R.E.        K.7.c.3.8 ) according to the situation
86th Inf. Bde.  K.6.c.4.5   advd. H.Q. LEDEGHEM STN.
88th    "       L.1.c.3.0      "    "   RAYMOND FARM.
497th Field Coy. R.E. K.8.a.5.3.
510th Field Coy. R.E. K.1.d.8.4.
1/2nd Mon. Pnr. Regt. J.5.d.3.9.

(d) <u>DRESS</u>

Fighting Order.
Leather Jerkins
Waterproof sheets
The day's rations
50 Rounds S.A.A.

(e) <u>PACKS</u>

These will be dumped at the present H.Q. under Spr Hames. (with two days rations.)

(f) <u>BICYCLES</u>

Ref. para 6(a). No.3 Section Cycles will be dumped at K.8.a.2.2 in charge of Spr. HAMES.

No.s 1, 2. & 4 Section Cycles will accompany section forward provided state of roads permits

If not, they will be left in charge of Spr Hames at K.8.a.2.2.

(g) <u>REPORTS</u> Completion of all work will be reported immediately to C.R.E. & O.C. Report Centre will be established as under :-

Advanced Div. Exchange   K.6.c.central.

The main Div. route will be extended by cable wagon via K.12.d.16 - KLEPHOEK - SOUTH OF LEDEGHEM - OVERHEULE - C.7.c - G.8.c & d to SALINES keeping in touch with 86 & 88 Inf. Bde. H.Q.

7.

(h). **Medical Arrangements.**

Regimental Aid Post. K. 12. 3. 2. 3.
Advanced Dressing Station K. 11. 3. 6. 5.

No 10 Please acknowledge

Copy No 1 — Lieut Jewson
" 2 — " Gillespie
" 3 — O.C. 497th Field Coy R.E.
" 4 — Lieut Elliott
" 5 — CRE
" 6 — C.S.M.
" 7 — Lieut Allan
" 8 — File
" 9 — War Diary

Extract para 6. O.C. 17th Bde.
RFA

J. Hines Capt R.E.
O.C.
497TH (KENT) FIELD CO: R.E.

## Ammendments

Ref. Para (8) Only one Pontoon Wagon will be attached to 455th Field Coy. The other pontoon wagon will be loaded with trestle equipment as no extra trestle wagon is being attached to the Coy.

Codes
~~29 Div.~~ — POLA
CRE — POFU
497 — ZOQI
455 — ROQA
510 — SORI
88 I.B. — MALO
86 I.B. — BANU
87 I.B. — MAJU
MONS — NUFE

13" Batt
DA — HAWI
A Battery

"A"

TRANSPORT.

| TRANSPORT | LOAD | STARTING POINT | TIME READY TO MOVE FORWARD ON "J" DAY. | GUIDE | DESTINATION | | REMARKS |
|---|---|---|---|---|---|---|---|
| | | | | | PLACE | UNIT. | |
| 1/2ND MONMOUTH REGT 5 LIMBERS | WHEEL BARROWS SPIKES NAILS. SANDBAGS ETC. | MACHINE GUN SIDING | ZERO + 1 HOUR | "C" COY. MONS. REGT. | HELL FIRE CORNER | 497TH (KENT) FIELD CO, R.E. LIEUT ELLIOTT. | Limbers will not move until orders are received from 497th Field Co. R.E. These limbers will report to ORILLA DUMP 2-30 P.M. "J" day and when loaded will proceed to MACHINE GUN SIDING to "C" Coy Camp. Horses will return to Horse Lines |
| 497TH (KENT) FIELD CO, R.E. PACK ANIMALS. | BOARDS FOR "B" TRACK SANDBAGS. | INFANTRY BARRACKS, YPRES. | ZERO + 1 HOUR. | NO. 1 SECTION | TRACK B | 497TH (KENT)FIELD CO, R.E. LIEUT. GILLESPIE | Pack animals will report INFANTRY BARRACKS 7-30 P.M. on "J" day. Mules & drivers to be accommodated at Barracks J/J night and to move forward under orders of O.C. No.1 Section. |
| TRESTLE WAGONS 6 HORSE TEAMS. | SERVICE TRESTLES. | MACHINE GUN SIDING | ZERO + 2 HOUR. | CAPT LINES | CULVERT I.18.a.27. | 497TH (KENT) FIELD CO, R.E. SERGT LUXFORD. | Wagons will not move until orders are received from O.C. 497th Field Co R.E. After delivery of trestles wagons will come under orders of O.C. No. 1 Section. |
| TRESTLE WAGON H. HORSES G.S. WAGON 4 HORSES. | SLABS. | HORSE LINES | 11-0 A.M. | MOUNTED N.C.O. | HOOGE | 497TH (KENT) FIELD CO.R.E. NO.1 SECTION. | In the event of any attention. LIEUT. JEWSON will give further orders. |

497th (Kent) Field Co. R.E.
Addendum to Operation Order No. 2.

Para. 12. No. 4 Section, 497th (Kent) Field Co R.E. } will assemble in
2 Platoons, 1/2nd Monmouth Pioneers } MOAT LANE about
T.M. B } Point I.15.b.2.5.
} between 1 and 3/4
} hr. before Zero.

Para 14. Capt. Turner of Monmouth Pioneers will be at
Advance Bde. H.Q. ~~I.16.a.5.8.~~ GORDON HOUSE I.15.b.4.5. and will let O.C. No. 4
Section know when to go forward.

Tools, Stores etc. Nos 1 and 4 Sections will take forward
5 and 10 buckets respectively.
   All tools etc will be delivered as soon
after dusk as possible at the INFANTRY BARRACKS
on the 27th inst.
   Nails will be carried forward as follows.
No. 1 Section & Pioneers, 1 cwt 6" and 1/2 cwt 8"
No 4    "      "      "    1  "  6"
   The 5 Limbers mentioned in para 6 will
take forward the following.-
   20 wheelbarrows
   4,000 sandbags
   7" and 9" spikes, 2 cwt each.
   6"  "  8" nails 2 cwt each.
   1 Limber load of stone in sandbags.

Runners. The "B" team, other than those mentioned in para 13.
will act as runners (cycle) from Coy. H.Q. to Machine
Gun Siding.
   Capt Lines will be at H.Q. of 510th Field Co R.E. This
must be reconoitred.

Reconoitring. Section Officers will reconnoitre the exits from YPRES in
Appendix "B"

Completion of Dayswork. The R.E. and Pioneers will return to their
billets on completion of work & be prepared to move their
camps on I plus 1 day.

Horse Lines. Company Horse Lines will be located at their
present location. A.29.d.7.3. & if ordered forward will move to
H.10.d.90.65.

MAJOR R.E.

# SECRET

## YPRES & GHELUVELT

— LEGEND —

Roads at present being maintained ―――
Roads to be maintained as per field engineers
(on the first line of 10 days) ―――

For foot traffic ........
Roads to be marked as for foot traffic tracks  - - - -
Proposed extension of tramline
Direction of traffic

Scale 1:10,000

To CRE
29th Division

Herewith War Diary for
October 1918, and Appendix "A"

J W Lines Capt R.E.
for MAJOR, R.E.
O.C. 497TH (KENT) FIELD CO. R.E.

SECRET    Copy    APPENDIX B

Sections ~~Units~~ will all reconnoitre every exit from YPRES in order that working parties may be able to get out quickly in case the route by which they had intended taking is under heavy shell fire.

The following are some of the exits known:-

1. LILLE GATE   I.14.a.85.10.
2. ISLAND BRIDGE.   I.14.a.4.2.
3. SALLY PORT, 2 Bridges. I.8.d.1.2. and I.8.d.1.3.
4. MENIN GATE   I.8. central.
5. Bridge   I.14.b.30.35 (doubtful)
6. DIXMUDE GATE   I.14.b.1.8.
7. I.7d.6.0.
8. Railway Station Road. I.13.b.0.7

26-9-18.

(Sd) R.N.A. Macaulay
Lt. Col. R.E.
C.R.E. 29th DIV.

Army Form C. 2118

497 Fd Coy R.E.

# WAR DIARY
## INTELLIGENCE SUMMARY
(Erase heading not required.)

Instructions regarding War Diaries and Intelligence Summaries are contained in F. S. Regs., Part II and the Staff Manual respectively. Title Pages will be prepared in manuscript.

| Place | Date | Hour | Summary of Events and Information | Remarks and references to Appendices |
|---|---|---|---|---|
| GLENCORSE WOOD J.14.a.3.6 | 1-10-18 | | Making double roadway from CLAPHAM JUNCTION to J.20.t.8-9 | 9MR |
| | 2-10-18 to 3-10-18 | | Coy. Working on main Road in Spare J.14. Transport moves up to Coy. | 9MR |
| | 4-10-18 | | Making accommodation for a battalion at WESTHOEK | 9MR |
| | 5-10-18 | | " " " " | Lt. CLEVELY proceeded to ROUEN for Course at R.E.F.S. 9MR |
| | 6-10-18 | | " " " " | 9MR |
| | 7-10-18 | | 3 Sections " 1 Section moves to J.7.a.5.7 and works under O.C. 510th Field Coy. R.E. | 9MR |
| 28/K.8.a.2.2 | to 9-10-18 | | | 9MR |
| | 10-10-18 | | Coy. moves to 28/K.8.a.2.2 | |
| | 11-10-18 to 12-10-18 | | 1 Section on Advanced D.H.Q. 1 Section on H.Q. for 88th Bde. 1 Section on H.Q. for R.F.A. + 1 Section on Infantry Bridge over steam in Square L.7.C. | 9MR |

# WAR DIARY
## INTELLIGENCE SUMMARY

Army Form C. 2118.

| Place | Date | Hour | Summary of Events and Information | Remarks and references to Appendices |
|---|---|---|---|---|
| OOSTHOEK | 13/10/18 | | MAJOR E.F. KNIGHT M.C. R.E. proceeded on leave to U.K. CAPT G.E. LINES R.E. assumed command of Coy. | M.L. |
| LEDEGHEM | 14/10/18 | | LT. B.C. ALLAN R.E. rejoined Coy. from leave U.K. Coy. made preparations for offensive. Coy. less No. 3 Section moved forward shortly after zero to near DADIZEELE to assist orders. | Appendix A |
| | | | No. 3 Section attached to 13th Battery 17 Bde. RFA for purpose of assisting them forward with advance. No. 2 Section on water taking and notice boarding. No. 1 and 4 sections in reserve. LT. ELLIOTT on reconnaissance. Coy. went into bivouac at MARKERSTING PM. | M.L. |
| SALINES | 15/10/18 | | No. 1 Sections on reserve for tractor bridges if necessary. No. 2 section water taking and notice boarding. No. 3 attacked 13th Battery. LT. ELLIOTT reconnaissance. | M.L. |
| SALINES | 16/10/18 | | No. 1 making barrel pier rafts and paddles for LYS. No. 2 water taking and notice boards. No. 3 attd 13th Battery R.F.A. No. 4 water taking. Reconnaissance continued. | M.L. |
| SALINES | 17/10/18 | | No. 3 rejoined Coy. No. 2 making barrel pier rafts in daytime. No. 1 attempted to get barrel rafts floated down to mouth of HEULEBEEK but could not owing to gas. No. 4 taking into trailer transport. Reconnaissance continued. LT. ALLAN admitted hospital. No. 3 | M.L. |
| SALINES | 18/10/18 | | No. 3 ad to building barrel pier bridges at HEULE DUMP. No. 1 in reserve. No. 2 floated barrel rafts to mouth of HEULEBEEK. In evening No. 1 attempted to get rafts portée across LYS for purpose of tempty patrol to find out if enemy still held opposite bank. M.G. fire at close range this was not possible. CAPT LINES recommended operations to be postponed — provide pontoon bridge. Bright moonlight. | M.L. |

Army Form C. 2118.

# WAR DIARY
## INTELLIGENCE SUMMARY.
*(Erase heading not required.)*

| Place | Date | Hour | Summary of Events and Information | Remarks and references to Appendices |
|---|---|---|---|---|
| SALINES | 19/10/18 | | No 4 built another travel pier bridge and loaded same on to G.S. wagons. No 3 attacked across LYS | |
| | | | by 4 ASST F.G. RE. No 3 at about 17.30 ran half pontoon ferry to HANTS. & foot | |
| | | | below COURTRAI. No 2 at about 23.00 ran travel pier raft across LYS at about | |
| | | | H21C87. No 1 at about 22.30 erected infantry in file travel pier bridge | |
| | | | across LYS at H21C87. 88th & Oth Bde crossed river on these bridges and opened Att | M.L. |
| | | | on Rly. thro' H.22. | |
| CUERNE | 20/10/18 | | Coy. moved to near CUERNE in afternoon. No 4 active embd on water testing & | |
| | | | extr. loading. LT. JENSON on reconnaissance. No 1, 2, action returned to billets | |
| | | | at SOURES after completion of bridge, pushed up & moved into billets at | |
| | | | CUERNE. Guards were left on both rafts and bridge. | M.L. |
| STACEGHEM | 21/10/18 | | Coy. moved to STACEGHEM in afternoon. No 1 and part of 3 making temporary | |
| | | | repairs to culvert under COURTRAI–BUSSUYT canal at H30d.5.4 in evening | |
| | | | No 2 on water testing. No 4 on active loading. No 3 remainder reconnaissance. | M.L. |
| " | 22/10/18 | | No 4 finish relief on culvert repair. No 1 second relief on culvert erecting 50% trusses | |
| | | | No 2 water testing and active loads. No 3 in reserve. | M.L. |
| " | 23/10/18 | | No 1 on repairs to culvert. No 2 water testing. No 3 dismantling foot bridge | M.L. |

# WAR DIARY
## INTELLIGENCE SUMMARY.
*(Erase heading not required.)*

Army Form C. 2118.

| Place | Date | Hour | Summary of Events and Information | Remarks and references to Appendices |
|---|---|---|---|---|
| STE. EGH E.M. | 24/10/18 | | No. 3 completed culvert. No. 4 glazing windows D.HQ. Nos 2 and 1 looking wagons. | A.P.L. |
| " | 25/10/18 | | Closed Rachie with German Pontoon bridge. Clearing of transport continued. Practice with German Pontoon equipt. Ladders to 65th F.Co. R.E. Wagons loaded. | A.P.L. |
| RISQUONS-TOUT | 26/10/18 | | Company marched with 88 2/f Bde to Willets at RISQUONS-TOUT (near MOUSCRON). Divisional Commander inspected. | A.P.L. |
| CROIX | 27/10/18 | | Company marched with 88 2/f Bde to Willets at Chemical who CROIX. Southwest of ROUBAIX. | A.P.L. |
| " | 28/10/18 | | Company working with 10 C.Ry.Co. on Railway Triangle, LILLE. Taking up damaged track & sleepers and relaying same. | A.P.L. |
| " | 29/10/18 | | Work on Railway continued. Laying track. | A.P.L. |
| " | 30/10/18 | | Coy. less No. 4 section working on Railway. Grading deviation. No. 4 section inspections deficiencies taken transport cleaned. MAJOR E.F. KNIGHT M.C. R.E. rejoined Coy. from leave and assumed Command of Company. | A.P.L. |
| " | 31/10/18 | | Coy. less No. 1 Section working on Railway. No. 1 Section on No. 4 on 30/10/18. | A.P.L. |

[signature] MAJOR R.E.
[signature] MAJOR R.E.
O.C. 497TH (KENT) FIELD CO. R.E.

CONFIDENTIAL

WAR DIARY.

of

497 (KENT) FIELD COY RE

From 1/11/18 to 30/11/18

VOLUME No. XXXVIII

ORIGINAL

Army Form C. 2118.

# WAR DIARY
## or
## INTELLIGENCE SUMMARY.
*(Erase heading not required.)*

Instructions regarding War Diaries and Intelligence Summaries are contained in F. S. Regs., Part II and the Staff Manual respectively. Title pages will be prepared in manuscript.

| Place | Date | Hour | Summary of Events and Information | Remarks and references to Appendices |
|---|---|---|---|---|
| (ROIX | 1/11/18 to 5/11/18 | | (3 sections working on railway under 10th Can. R. Batln. (1 section inspection drill etc. | |
| " | 6/11/18 | | Company moved by road to 29/T.12.a.9.7. | |
| 29/T.12.a.9.7 | 7/11/18 | | Reconnoitring the river ESCAUT. Coy Gives Transport move to 29/U.30.a.9.9. Transport move to 29/0.26.b.6.3. No 472028/4/41 Saprs Sh. RES. & N° 526226/4/41 GUILLIM W.M. wounded. | EnR |
| 29/U.30.a.4.7 | 8/11/18 | | Transport moved up to the Company. 2 Sections make infantry bridge across the river ESCAUT at BOSSUIT. 2 Section repair infantry float bridge near the river ESCAUT at 29/U.24.b.55 & 29/U.30.a.B.3. | |
| 29/U.30.a.4.7 | 9/11/18 | | Company moved to 29/U.23.c.2.8. | |
| 29/U.30.a.4.7 | 10/11/18 | | Company less transport moved to CELLES. (37/D.16.b.6.6) 1 section doing transport work to lorrybridge at CELLES. 1 " erect Service truck bridge at 37/C.6.b.1.7. 2 " repair road between HELCHIN & CELLES. | |

**ORIGINAL**

Army Form C. 2118.

# WAR DIARY
## or
## INTELLIGENCE SUMMARY.
*(Erase heading not required.)*

Instructions regarding War Diaries and Intelligence Summaries are contained in F.S. Regs., Part II. and the Staff Manual respectively. Title pages will be prepared in manuscript.

| Place | Date | Hour | Summary of Events and Information | Remarks and references to Appendices |
|---|---|---|---|---|
| CELLES | 10/11/18 | | 2 Sections erecting Lorry bridge at CELLES | |
| | | | 1 " Repairs silk to Lorry bridge at 37/C.6.6.17 | |
| | | | 1 " repair road between HELCHIN & CELLES. Tonight (one Coy.) | |
| | 11/11/18 | | Armistice came into force. Hostilities suspended from 11:00 | |
| | 12/11/18 | | 1 Section complete Lorry bridge at CELLES | |
| | | | 2 " repair road at E.18.d.59 | |
| | | | 1 " crater blown diversion at Crater 37/D.17.d.2.6. | M |
| | 13/11/18 | | 2 " repair culvert at E.18.d.5.9 & repair roads. | |
| | | | 1 " removing shells from roads & junction. | |
| CELLES | 14/11/18 | | Company move to FLOBECQ | |
| FLOBECQ | 15/11/18 | | " " LESSINES 38/G.17.a.4.1 | |
| LESSINES | 16/11/18 | | Kit inspections etc. Drill | |
| | 17/11/18 | | Cleaning wagons etc | |
| | 18/11/18 | | Company attached to 98th Inf Brigade. Advance to Germany commences | |
| | | | Company moves to MARCQ (BRUSSELS 6.4.9 21.32) | |
| MARCQ | 19-20/11/18 | | Reconnoitring for and running demolitions | |

ORIGINAL

Army Form C. 2118.

# WAR DIARY
## or
## INTELLIGENCE SUMMARY.
(Erase heading not required.)

Instructions regarding War Diaries and Intelligence Summaries are contained in F. S. Regs., Part II. and the Staff Manual respectively. Title pages will be prepared in manuscript.

| Place | Date | Hour | Summary of Events and Information | Remarks and references to Appendices |
|---|---|---|---|---|
| MARCQ | 21/11/18 | | Company marches to CLABECQ. (Brussels. 6 & 4 D. a 18) | 1 |
| CLABECQ | 22/11/18 | | Drill & games | |
| " | 23/11/18 | | Company moves to COUTURE ST GERMAIN (Brussels. 6 A.F. 74 H) | |
| COUTURE ST GERMAIN | 24/11/18 | | Inspection | |
| " | 25/11/18 | | Company moves to MOUSTY (Brussels 6. 5 G. 7 B. 9 A). Div Band & brass Comp ---- 2/Lt | |
| MOUSTY | 26/11/18 | | Cleaning wagons. | |
| " | 27/11/18 | | Company moves to LERINNES. (Brussels 6. 51. 67. 50.) | |
| LERINNES | 28/11/18 | | Company moves to HARLUE (Brussels 6.5.K 94.32.) L Gillespie posted to | |
| | | | Coy. 2/Lt Bryan join the company from R.E.B.D. | |
| HARLUE | 29/11/18 | | Company moves to LA HÉSBAYE (Liege 7. 68. 67. 52.) | |
| LA HESBAYE | 30/11/18 | | Company moves to ELLEMELLE (Marche 9. 1.F.32.63.) | 1 |

S/Kund

497th (Kent) Fd Co RE
Dec 1918.   WO 95/34

**Army Form C. 2118.**

# WAR DIARY
## or
## INTELLIGENCE SUMMARY.
*(Erase heading not required.)*

Instructions regarding War Diaries and Intelligence Summaries are contained in F. S. Regs., Part II. and the Staff Manual respectively. Title pages will be prepared in manuscript.

| Place | Date | Hour | Summary of Events and Information | Remarks and references to Appendices |
|---|---|---|---|---|
| I.F 32.6.3 | 1/12/18 | | Bty moved to SOUGNE (I.I 49.7.9. (MARCHE 9)) Corpl Barrett S. accidentally killed | |
| SOUGNE | 2/12/18 | | (drowned) before Bty moved off | |
| " | 3/12/18 | | Inspection Parade and cleaning transport | |
| " | 4/12/18 | | Rest and fixture | |
| LES COMBLES | 5/12/18 | | Bty moved to LES COMBLES (I.J.56.88 (MARCHE 9)) | |
| BÜRNENVILLE | 6/12/18 | | Bty moved to BÜRNENVILLE, GERMANY (I.L.9&16 (MARCHE 9)) Bty crossed frontier 14:15 | |
| LAGER EISENBORN | 7/12/18 | | Bty moved LAGER EISENBORN. Billeted in German Artillery Training Centre Barracks | |
| IMGENBROICH | 8/12/18 | | Bty moved to IMGENBROICH | |
| VLATTEN | 9/12/18 | | Bty moved to VLATTEN | |
| ERP | 10/12/18 | 11.7.12 | Bty moved to ERP | |
| BACHEM | 11/12/18 | | Bty moved to BACHEM, near COLOGNE | |
| " | 12/12/18 | | Drill, cleaning transport and equipment | |
| " | 13/12/18 | | Bty take part in march through COLOGNE with 88th Brigade passing Corps Commander at saluting base on HOHENZOLLERN BRIDGE. Bty moved into billets at MÜLHEIM | |
| MÜLHEIM | 14/12/18 | | Kit Inspection and Rest | |
| " | 15/12/18 | | Bty move to GRUNAU | |

# WAR DIARY
## or
## INTELLIGENCE SUMMARY.
*(Erase heading not required.)*

Army Form C. 2118.

Instructions regarding War Diaries and Intelligence Summaries are contained in F. S. Regs., Part II. and the Staff Manual respectively. Title pages will be prepared in manuscript.

| Place | Date | Hour | Summary of Events and Information | Remarks and references to Appendices |
|---|---|---|---|---|
| GRUNAU | 16/12/18 | | Drill and P.T. Coy came under of C.O.R.E. 29th Division | |
| " | 17/12/18 | | Drill P.T. and Lecture | |
| " | 18/12/18 | | Drill and P.T. | |
| " | 19/12/18 | | Coy moved to BURSCHEID. First billeting in Bridgehead. | |
| BURSCHEID | 20/12/18 | | Inspection Parade and Coy came under Regimental Orders | |
| " | 21/12/18 | | Improving Coy Billets and roading to Horse Lines. Lieut D. GILLESPIE reported back from leave | S/R |
| " | 22/12/18 | | Improving Coy Billets and Horse Lines and constructing Rifle Range | |
| " | 23/12/18 | | Improving Coy Billets and Horse Lines and constructing Rifle Range. 16 Reinforcements to join Coy | |
| " | 24/12/18 | | Improving Coy Billets and Horse Lines and constructing Rifle Range. 2 Reinforcements to join Coy | |
| " | 25/12/18 | | Christmas Day. No Xmas Dinner. | |
| " | 26/12/18 | | Making Rifle Range and Water Point | |
| " | 27/12/18 | | Coys. Tour of Duty commenced unloading of R.E. Stores from town. | |
| " | 28/12/18 | | Unloading of R.E. Stores from town, making W/tar boards and improving Horse Lines | |
| " | 29/12/18 | | Church Parade and unloading of R.E. Stores from town | |
| " | 30/12/18 | | Making water trough. Erecting Cook House and attention to Stables | |
| " | 31/12/18 | | Finishing water trough. Erecting Latrines & Cook House. Work on Rifle Range. Improving Horse Lines. | |

*(Signed) M.N____, Major R.E.*
*O.C. 497 (Kent) Field Coy R.E.*

RHINE ARMY
SOUTHERN DIVISION
LATE 29TH DIVISION

497TH (KENT) FLD COY R.E.

JAN - OCT 1919

2066 & 2084

CONFIDENTIAL

WAR DIARY.

of

497th FIELD COY. R.E.

From 1/1/19 to 31/1/19

VOLUME No. 40

# WAR DIARY
## or
## INTELLIGENCE SUMMARY

*(Erase heading not required.)*

Army Form C. 2118

Instructions regarding War Diaries and Intelligence Summaries are contained in F. S. Regs., Part II. and the Staff Manual respectively. Title Pages will be prepared in manuscript.

| Place | Date | Hour | Summary of Events and Information | Remarks and references to Appendices |
|---|---|---|---|---|
| BURSCHIED. | 12/1/19. | | Church Parade. | |
| | 13/1/19. | | Work same as 11/1/19. Capt Akin return from leave. Sgt AITKEN & Spr Gibson proceed to U.K. for demobilization. | |
| | 14/1/19 to 15/1/19. | | 1 Section on Duty. 1 Section work in billets. return for D.R. & Rifle Range. Section on detachment same on 10/1/19. 1 Section a Rifle Range. 1 Section in billets. 2 sections on detached. | |
| | 16/1/19. | | Same as 15/1/19. | |
| | 17/1/19. 18/1/19. | | Section Cos at BURSCHIED births, 2 sections on detachment work. Coy & 2 Sections drill + clear hills, 2 sections on detachment | – SJR |
| | 19/1/19. 20/1/19. | | work as for 16/1/19. Church Parade. | |
| | 21/1/19. | | Same as 16/1/19. | |
| | 22/1/19. 23/1/19. | | Same as 15/1/19. | |
| | 24/1/19. | | Same as 16/1/19 + baths + Stores | |

**Army Form C. 2118**

# WAR DIARY
## or
## INTELLIGENCE SUMMARY
*(Erase heading not required.)*

| Place | Date | Hour | Summary of Events and Information | Remarks and references to Appendices |
|---|---|---|---|---|
| BURSCHIED COLOGNE BRIDGEHEAD | 1-1-19 | | 1 Section making Rifle Range by Brickworks. 1 Section cleaning Wagons. 2 Sections improving billets & latrines. | |
| | 2-1-19 3-1-19 4-1-19 | | Ditto. Plus made Russimer. Delouser at WERMELS-KIRCHEN. | |
| | | | 1 Section made Rifle Range, 2 Section Improving billets & latrines, also Delouser. 1 Section (complete with transport) under Lt ELLIOT. moves to billets à BERG GLADBACH. to work for D.A. & A.S.C. | |
| | 5/1/19 to 7/1/19 | | 1 Section on Duty. 1 Section on Rifle Range 1 Section on Coy Billets & 1 Section moving erecting stables for DA + ASC at BERG GLADBACH. – NB | |
| | 8/1/19 | | 1 Section on Rifle Range. 2 Section on Coy Billets & Latrines for SA. | |
| | | | 1 Section working for DA + ASC at BERG GLADBACH | |
| | 9/1/19 & 10/1/19 | | 1 Section on Rifle Range. 1 Section on Billets & latrines for S.A. 1 Section working at BERG GLADBACH made 125 Begony (Aero Transport) moves to PAFFRATH, also & erects Bunches, latrines etc for 38th Bde R.F.A. as have lost their CRE inspects billets, latrines or detachment work. | |

# WAR DIARY
## or
## INTELLIGENCE SUMMARY

Army Form C. 2118

| Place | Date | Hour | Summary of Events and Information | Remarks and references to Appendices |
|---|---|---|---|---|
| BURSCHEID | 25/1/19 | | 2 Section's Drill & Clean billets, 2 Sections in abluhood room | |
| | 26/1/19 | | as 10/1/19. Coy Comd. & Spr Daniels proceed to UK for demobilisation. Church Parade. | |
| | 27/1/19 | | Same as 16/1/19. in Lt Jensen relieves Lt Whit at BERG GLADBACH. | 9/12 |
| | 28/1/19 | | Lt Cleverly returns from leave. 1 Section duty, otherwise work same as 27/1/19. 1 Section returns fm PAFFRATH. | |
| | 29/1/19 | | 1 Section on duty. 1 Section on Rifle Range. 1 Section in billets. 1 Section at BERG GLADBACH working for D.A.D. & S.C. Lt Elliot proceeds on leave | |
| | 30/1/19 | | | |
| | 31/1/19 | | Work same as 29/1/19. | |

signature

MAJOR, R.E.
O.O. 497TH (KENT) FIELD CO; R.E.

CONFIDENTIAL

WAR DIARY,

of

497 Field Coy. RE

From 1/2/19 to 28/2/19

VOLUME No. 41

# WAR DIARY or INTELLIGENCE SUMMARY

Army Form C. 2118

| Place | Date | Hour | Summary of Events and Information | Remarks and references to Appendices |
|---|---|---|---|---|
| BURSCHEID GERMANY | 1/2/19 | | No 4 Section (LT. JENSON) on detachment at BERG-GLADBACH. Practice parade for G.O.C.'s Inspection. Coys. independently, then combined under C.R.E. Dismounted portion of Coy. Baths. | ML |
| " | 2/2/19 | | Conservancy. | ML |
| " | 3/2/19 | | G.O.C.'s Inspection. Return of British, French & Belgium decoration presented by G.O.C. | ML |
| " | 4/2/19 | | Coy. come on duty. Work in hand – ablution shed, screening horse lines, cooking etc. | ML |
| " | 5/2/19 | | Coy. on duty. Work as 4/2/19. | ML |
| " | 6/2/19 | | Coy. on duty. " " " | ML |
| " | 7/2/19 | | Work as 4/2. Baths. | ML |
| " | 8/2/19 | | Conservancy. One hour's drill. 25 O.R. proceed to U.K. on Demobilisation. | ML |
| " | 9/2/19 | | Church Parade. LT. F.D. CLEVELY proceeded to U.K. tried for by Ministry of Munitions. 3 O.R. proceed on leave to U.K. | ML |
| " | 10/2/19 | | Coy. work as 4/2 + also trucking driving filter. | ML |
| " | 11/2/19 | | as 10/2. | ML |
| " | 12/2/19 | | Coy. on duty. As 10/2 + divine service. | ML |
| " | 13/2/19 | | No 3 Section joined No 4 at BERG-GLADBACH. Work on new dining hall. | ML |

Army Form C. 2118

# WAR DIARY or INTELLIGENCE SUMMARY
(Erase heading not required.)

Instructions regarding War Diaries and Intelligence Summaries are contained in F. S. Regs., Part II. and the Staff Manual respectively. Title Pages will be prepared in manuscript.

| Place | Date | Hour | Summary of Events and Information | Remarks and references to Appendices |
|---|---|---|---|---|
| BURSCHEID GERMANY | 14/2/19 | | Coy. on duty. Baths. Work as usual. | M. |
| " | 15/2/19 | | Conservancy. Drill 11:30 – 12:30 | M. |
| " | 16/2/19 | | Church parade. No 3 & 4 Sections at B. GLADBACH. | M. |
| " | 17/2/19 | | Coy. erecting new stables in STATION RD. BURSCHEID. Coy. Cookhouse, excavating for pipe line to ablution sheds. Mess dining room. Civilian labourers helping on stables. | M. |
| | | | LT. G.M. ELLIOTT R.E. rejoined from leave to U.K. | |
| " | 18/2/19 | | Work as 17th + Brivic's [Drivers] lunks. | M. |
| " | 19/2/19 | | Work as 18th. LT. ELLIOTT proceeded to B. GLADBACH to take over from LT. JEWSON. | M. |
| " | 20/2/19 | | Coy. comes on duty. Work as 18th. | M. |
| " | 21/2/19 | | Coy. on duty. Work as 18th. ‖ LT. BRYAN rejoins Coy. from Hospital. ‖ LT. JEWSON rejoins Coy. from B. GLADBACH. | M. |
| " | 22/2/19 | | ‖ LT. A.N. PATRICK R.E. (R) joins Coy. from R.E. Base Depot. No 1 & 2 Sections, Conservancy. Baths. Rifle & Gas drill. | M. |
| " | 23/2/19 | | Church Parade. | M. |
| " | 24/2/19 | | No 3 Section Baths. B. GLADBACH. Remainder of Coy. Sunday driven billets, erecting Coy. & Drivers Cookhouses, new stables, pipe line for ablution shed. No 3 & 4 at 3. GLADBACH erecting stables, Gun parks, repairing stables etc. | M. |

# WAR DIARY
## or
## INTELLIGENCE SUMMARY
*(Erase heading not required.)*

Army Form C. 2118

| Place | Date | Hour | Summary of Events and Information | Remarks and references to Appendices |
|---|---|---|---|---|
| BURSCHEID | 25/2/19 | | Work as 24th. | M |
| GERMANY | 26/2/19 | | Do. Do. | M |
| " | 27/2/19 | | Do. Do. | M |
| " | 28/2/19 | | Do. Do. and baths. 1 Lt. R.F. Ellingworth D.C.M. R.E. joined Coy. from 7th (Horrel) Pontoon Park | M |

J. Munio Capt. R.E.
O.C. 497 P.Co. R.E.

29th Dr.

CONFIDENTIAL

WAR DIARY.

of

497th Field Coy RE

From 1/5/19 to 31/5/19

VOLUME No. 44.

Army Form C. 2118.

# WAR DIARY
## or
## INTELLIGENCE SUMMARY
(Erase heading not required.)

497 (KENT) FIELD Co. Y. R.E.

| Place | Date | Hour | Summary of Events and Information | Remarks and references to Appendices |
|---|---|---|---|---|
| BURSCHEID Germany | 1/6/19 | | Work continued on Hutting, Ranges etc – work in hand, Officers Mess at DALBRINGHAUSEN, do. at STUMPF, do at DHUM, rifle range at DELLBRUCK, small jobs in 3rd Southern Inf. Bde area. | |
| | 2/6/19 | 9/OC | Visited DELLBRUCK range. | |
| | 3/6/19 | | Visited DALBRINGHAUSEN, STUMPF and DHUM with officers in charge. 20 Infantry from 3rd Southern Bde attached to unit for employment on lines to relieve Sappers now employed there owing to low strength of drivers. | |
| | 4/6/19 | | Rest day | |
| | 6/7/19 to 9/6/19 | | Work continued on above jobs. Training of Inf. attached to Horse lines commenced, with a view to transfer of suitable men as Drivers R.E. Work commenced on officers mess Dhunn. | |
| | 10/6/19 | | " " | |
| | 11/6/19 | | Training and interior economy. Rest day. | |

# WAR DIARY or INTELLIGENCE SUMMARY

Army Form C. 2118.

| Place | Date | Hour | Summary of Events and Information | Remarks and references to Appendices |
|---|---|---|---|---|
| BURSCHEID Germany | 12/5/19 | | Work continued. Visited proposed 400 rang at WIRMELSKIRCHEN with C.E. II Corps + Bde. Major 3rd Southern Inf. Bde. Work commenced on Disinfector, Wermelskirchen. | |
| | 13/5/19 | | Company brought up to war establishment in dismounted ranks, with a view to possible active operations. Drafts received on 12.5.19 from 155 + 510 Field Coys R.E. Work on disinfector at WERMELSKIRCHEN continued. | |
| | 14/5/19 | | Visited DALBRINGHAUSEN, DHUM, STUMPF and WERMELSKIRCHEN with C.R.E. Progress satisfactory. | |
| | 15/5/19 | | Major R. Purcell, D.S.O. R.E. returned from leave & resumed command. O.C. inspected work in progress at BURSCHEID & inspected Regt Institute. Work on Disinfector. 1 Offr. & 24 O.R. (97 Field Coy. Pioneers) reported for work. | |
| | 16/5/19 | | Visited Dellbrouck Rifle Range with C.R.E. and Officers Instructional Class under 2/Lieut T.A. NEWMAN M.M. attd. 4 Offrs & 22 O.R. (Pioneers) detailed for Dethit. Visited work at DELLBROUCK & BERG GLADBACH. | |
| | 17/5/19 | | Work as usual. O.C. visited work at DELLBROUCK & BERG GLADBACK. Conveyancy carried out. | |
| | 18/5/19 | | Rest Day. Church Parade. O.C. & C.R.E. visited work at WERMELSKIRCHEN, DABRINGHAUSEN and DHUNN. | |

**Army Form C. 2118.**

# WAR DIARY
## or
## INTELLIGENCE SUMMARY
*(Erase heading not required.)*

| Place | Date | Hour | Summary of Events and Information | Remarks and references to Appendices |
|---|---|---|---|---|
| BERSHEID GERMANY. | 19/7/19 | | Work as usual. O.C visited Rifles Horse Wagon Lines. Pellenoy Rifle Range in afternoon. | |
| | 20/7/19 | | Work as usual. O.C visited workshops Regt Institutes | |
| | 21/7/19 | | O.C lectured to Officers Class BERG GLADBACH. Visited Coy Lines and Riding Classes. | |
| | 22/7/19 | | O.C visited work. Attended Conference with C.R.E. relative to Cookery moving forward if "Peace Treaty" were not signed. | |
| | 23/7/19 | | Work as usual. O.C visited Officer Class with C.R.E. to BERG GLADBACH — checked baker and criticised after checking. | |
| | 24/7/19 | | Work commenced on Disinfector DABRINGHAUSEN and Men's Hut STUMPF for M.G. Bath. | |
| | | | Work as usual. O.C checked baker of Officers Class. Visited stables & Billets. | |
| | 25/7/19 | | Work as usual. O.C visited work at DABRINGHAUSEN, STUMPF, DHUNN & WSRMELSKIRCHEN. | |

# WAR DIARY or INTELLIGENCE SUMMARY

Army Form C. 2118.

(Erase heading not required.)

| Place | Date | Hour | Summary of Events and Information | Remarks and references to Appendices |
|---|---|---|---|---|
| BURSCHEID GERMANY | 26/5 | | Conkers to Church. O.C. visited all work in progress with C.R.E. | |
| | 27/5 | | Work as usual. Work commenced on Officers Mess for M.G. Batt. at STUMPF. Army Commander visited. | |
| | 28/5 | | O.C. visited works. Shooting started with rifles. | |
| | 29/5 | | do — NCO's Range. O.C. visited Rifle Range DELLBROVER. | |
| | 30/5 | | O.C. visited work at BURSCHEID. | |
| | 31/5 | | Conkery for Coy H.Q.'s. Packing and Safety Drill carried out. Inspection of whole Miller. | |

Burscheid.
Germany.
31-5-19.

[signature]
MAJOR, R.E.
O.C. 497TH (KENT) FIELD CO: R.E.

29 DIV.

CONFIDENTIAL

WAR DIARY.

of

497 (KENT) FIELD COY. R.E.

From June 1st to June 30th

VOLUME No. 45.

**Army Form C. 2118.**

**JUNE PERIOD** — WAR DIARY or INTELLIGENCE SUMMARY
(Erase heading not required.)

No. 45

497/2 (KENT) FIELD COY. R.E.

| Place | Date | Hour | Summary of Events and Information | Remarks and references to Appendices |
|---|---|---|---|---|
| BURSCHEID, GERMANY. | 1/6/19 | | Church Service. O.C visited work in progress. | O.C. Lt Marshall sick leave 7 days. |
| | 2/6/19 | | Work as usual. O.C. visiting DELLBROUCK Rifle Range. | |
| | 3/6/19 | | Ceremonial Parade. Kings Birthday. Company reviewed by 1 officer & 35 O.R. | |
| | 4/6/19 | | O.C visited work at ABRINGHAUSEN, STUMPF & D HUNN. Company won FOOTBALL Competition 6-a-side. | |
| | 5/6/19 | | Work as usual. O.C visited work. | |
| | 6/6/19 | | " " | Leverken Divisional Race Meeting. 2 horses entered unplaced. |
| | 7/6/19 | | " " | |
| | 8/6/19 | | Church Service. Office routine. | |
| | 9/6/19 | | Holiday. | |
| | 10/6/19 | | Work as usual. O.C visited work. Engineer in Chief visited work in progress. Lt Leonard returned from leave. | Lt Leonard to 3rd Lauchen Infantry Brigade for escort to Germans to HANNOVER HUFE. (G.43.02.) Rifle Range. |

# WAR DIARY
## or
## INTELLIGENCE SUMMARY
*(Erase heading not required.)*

Army Form C. 2118.

| Place | Date | Hour | Summary of Events and Information | Remarks and references to Appendices |
|---|---|---|---|---|
| BURSCHEID GERMANY | 11/6/19 | | Work as usual. O.C. visited work. | |
| | 12/6/19 | | C.R.E. on leave. Major Mitchell D.S.O. R.E. assuming duties of C.R.E. | |
| | 13/6/19 | | Work as usual. O.C. visited all work in progress. | |
| | 14/6/19 | | O.C. visited Kesselsdahl with a view to combing with Company for training in fieldworks. | |
| | 15/6/19 | | Work as usual. O.C. visited work. | |
| | 16/6/19 | | Church parade. O.C. visited WITZHELDON for photographing. | |
| | | | Work as usual. O.C. visited Pioneer work. | |
| | 17/6/19 | 9.00 | Orders received 16th June 7-3. 2/Lt SWAINSTON returned from leave. Work as usual. Cooking stove. Detachment moved to held rehearsive in readiness to rejoin H.Q. Lieut GENOCHIO joined Detachment. Returned to Coy Headqs. 2/Lt PATRICK leave to U.K. | |
| | 18/6/19 | | | |
| | 19/6/19 | | Overhauling stores, packing surplus equipment inventories to move to Brigade Dump, HILGEN. C.R.E. returned from leave. | |
| | 20/6/19 | | Receiving Reports BURSCHEID allotted to Company. Surplus stores removed to HILGEN. | |

**Army Form C. 2118.**

**WAR DIARY**
or
**INTELLIGENCE SUMMARY**

*(Erase heading not required.)*

Instructions regarding War Diaries and Intelligence Summaries are contained in F.S. Regs., Part II. and the Staff Manual respectively. Title Pages will be prepared in manuscript.

| Place | Date | Hour | Summary of Events and Information | Remarks and references to Appendices |
|---|---|---|---|---|
| BURSCHEID GERMANY | 21/6/19 | | Packing Equipment & Stores for Advance. | |
| | 22/6/19 | | Company with transport proceeded on short Route march. Church Parade. O.C. visited sites for Pontooning with Pts. Tecontrell, Henochs, Lewington. | |
| | 23/6/19 | | Company standing by ready to advance. Packing of vehicle equipment commenced. | |
| | 24/6/19 | | As previous day. | |
| | 25/6/19 | | As previous day. | |
| | 26/6/19 | | As previous day. | |
| | 27/6/19 | | As previous day. Company hushed. | |
| | 28/6/19 | | Company Training Drill. Cricket Match with 610 Coy R.E. Result. WIN. | |
| | 29/6/19 | | Church Parade. | |
| | 30/6/19 | | Packing by section to move not on Detachment for work. | |
| | | | Peace Treaty signed on 28-6-19 NOT officially informed to-night of 3rd M.[?] | |

MAJOR, R.E.
O.C. 497TH (KENT) FIELD Coi R.E.

C.R.E.
Lauthi Dn.

Herewith Diary for month ending 31st July 1919.

3/7/19.

A. Russell
Major R.E.
O.C. 497.

**WAR DIARY**
or
**INTELLIGENCE SUMMARY** 407 2(KENT) FIELD COY. R.E.
(Erase heading not required.)

Army Form C. 2118.

| Place | Date | Hour | Summary of Events and Information | Remarks and references to Appendices |
|---|---|---|---|---|
| BURSCHEID GERMANY. | 7/1/19. | — | Sections paraded in halls and proceeded on Detachment.— No.1. SECTION. (2/Lt. R.TURNBULL.R.E.) 10.00 hr. STUMPF. No.2. SECTION. (2/Lt. H.I. SWAINSTON R.E.) 07.00 hr. DHUNN. No.4. SECTION. (Lt. A.M. GENOCHIO R.E.) 10.30 hr. DABRINGHAUSEN. No.3 SECTION. 6 N.C.Os then 07.00 hr. WERMELSKIRCHEN. 6 " 10.30 hr. DABRINGHAUSEN. Work on Rifle Range FINKENHOLL commenced. Repairs to Disinfector BERG GLADBACH completed. Capt H der PANET R.E. proceeded to ENGLAND for Course at S.M.E. CHATHAM. Lieut. R.TURNBULL R.E. returned from STUMPF and assumed duties of second in command. | |
| | 27/9. | | O.C. visited Sections on Detachment. #/Lt. A.R. PATRIO R.E. returned from leave and posted to No.1 SECTION. | |

**Army Form C. 2118.**

# WAR DIARY
## or
## INTELLIGENCE SUMMARY
*(Erase heading not required.)*

Instructions regarding War Diaries and Intelligence Summaries are contained in F.S. Regs, Part II. and the Staff Manual respectively. Title Pages will be prepared in manuscript.

| Place | Date | Hour | Summary of Events and Information | Remarks and references to Appendices |
|---|---|---|---|---|
| BURSCHEID | 3.7.19. | | O.C. visited work & detachment. | |
| GERMANY. | 4.7.19. | | Work as usual. | |
| | 5.7.19. | | Holiday. Mounted Sports in afternoon & Cricket Match with g.th Siloin Reg 1 (Pioneers). | |
| | 6.7.19. | | Work as usual. O.C. visited works. | |
| | 7.7.19. | | Church Parade. | |
| | 8.7.19. | | Work as usual. O.C. visited works. | |
| | 9.7.19. | | " " " " | |
| | 10.7.19 | | " " " " Disinfectors at WERMELSKIRCHEN completed & men sent to work on Rifle Range FINKENHOLL. | |
| | 11.7.19. | | Work as usual. O.C. visited works. | |
| | 12.7.19. | | " " " " | |
| | 13.7.19. | | Church Parade. | |
| | 14.7.19 | | Work as usual. — Large hut at STUMPF completed. 1 Offr & 30 O.R. Q.M. Scots Regt attached for cookery. RANGEN, q.HAUSEN and STUMPF. | |

# WAR DIARY
## INTELLIGENCE SUMMARY

Army Form C. 2118.

| Place | Date | Hour | Summary of Events and Information | Remarks and references to Appendices |
|---|---|---|---|---|
| BERGSCHEID GERMANY. | 15.7.19 | | Work as usual. O.C. visited work. | |
| | 16.7.19 | | " " | |
| | 17.7.19 | | " " | |
| | 18.7.19 | | " Disinfector completed at DABRINGHAUSEN. Men sent to work on completing Cookhouse at DABRINGHAUSEN. | |
| | 19.7.19 | | Holiday. Inspection of Mounted Section with vehicles. Brig. ever so early. | |
| | 20.7.19 | | 10/ Ponton. G.S. Wagon, No 2 Section limber, No 3 Section limber and cart, Church Parade. Orders received to cease work on Officers Mess at DHUNN, STUMPF and DABRINGHAUSEN. Nos 1 & 4 Sections proceed to Rail Cone MULHEIM and work ends. 15.7" Field Coy No.5. | |
| | 21.7.19 | | No 1 st Section proceeded to MULHEIM. No 2 Section took over work of Cookhouse at STUMPF and DABRINGHAUSEN. | |
| | 22.7.19 | | Work as usual. O.C. visited work. | |
| | 23.7.19 | | " " | |
| | 24.7.19 | | Company Raid. O.C. visited works. | |
| | 26.7.19 | | " " | |

# WAR DIARY or INTELLIGENCE SUMMARY

Army Form C. 2118.

| Place | Date | Hour | Summary of Events and Information | Remarks and references to Appendices |
|---|---|---|---|---|
| BURSCHEID, GERMANY. | 26/7/19 | | Sunday. Divt R.E. Sports. | |
| | 27/7/19 | | Church Parade. Coy. Fairhurst proceeded on P.T. & B.F. Course. Work as usual. | |
| | 28/7/19 | | O.C. Revised work with C.R.E. | |
| | 29/7/19 | | " O.C. revised work. | |
| | 30/7/19 | | " O.C. " " | |
| | 31/7/19 | | 1 mule destroyed. Corp. Baker leg through kick (No. 43). 1/Cpl Pariett R.E. detailed for attachment to 2nd London Infantry Brigade for 1 month. | |

MAJOR, R.E.
O.C. 497TH (KENT) FIELD Coy R.E.

CONFIDENTIAL

# ORIGINAL

## WAR DIARY

### OF

### 497TH FIELD COY R.E.

### FOR

### MONTH OF AUGUST 1919.

### VOLUME 47

**Army Form C. 2118.**

# WAR DIARY or INTELLIGENCE SUMMARY

(No. 47)

497th (Kent) Field Coy. R.E.

| Place | Date | Hour | Summary of Events and Information | Remarks and references to Appendices |
|---|---|---|---|---|
| BURSCHEID. GERMANY. | 1/7/19 | | Work carried on at STUMPF, DABRINGHAUSEN, KEMPEN & FINKENHOLL. 10 additional men sent to KALK. | |
| | 2/7/19 | | Work as usual. O.C. visited works. | |
| | 3/7/19 | | Church Parade. | |
| | 4/7/19 | | Holiday. | |
| | 5/7/19 | | Work as usual. O.C. visited works. | |
| | 6/7/19 | | " Enough finished at KEMPEN. | |
| | 7/7/19 | | " O.C. visited works. | |
| | 8/7/19 | | " South Division Tournament. | |
| | 9/7/19 | | " | |
| | 10/7/19 | | Church Parade. 7 Animals (4 horse, 3 mules) sent to Light Division Camb. SOLINGEN for sale. Lieut. H.I. SWAINSTON R.E. in charge. | |
| | 11/7/19 | | Lt. Turnbull R.E. assumes command of the Coy vice Major A. Rennell R.E. on Special leave to the U.K. | |
| | 12/7/19 | | Lt. H.I. Swainston R.E. relieves Lt. H.M. Genochio R.E. at KALK. | |

# WAR DIARY
## or
## INTELLIGENCE SUMMARY.

Army Form C. 2118.

| Place | Date | Hour | Summary of Events and Information | Remarks and references to Appendices |
|---|---|---|---|---|
| BURSCHEID | 13/7/19 | | Work as usual. O.C. visited units. | |
| GERMANY. | 14/7/19 | | Continues finished at STUMPH & DABRINGHAUSEN. O.C. visited PATTSCHEID have re-organised training camp site for pontooning. 1st Reinforcements included to u/c | |
| | 15/7/19 | | Pay parade. 1 officer & 4 men proceeded Army Reception Camp en route on draft for EGYPT. | |
| | 16/7/19 | | Work as usual. | |
| | 17/7/19 | | Church parade. L/Sniveliston R.E. + detachment returned from KALK. | |
| | 18/7/19 | | Army Horse Show MERHEIM. Major L. Russell returned from leave Horse & our Lorry & chr. Leschi Dr. Army Hymn show. Rest as usual. | |
| | 19/7/19 | | | |
| | 20/7/19 | | | |
| | 21/7/19 | | 100 + Rifle Range at FINKENHOFF completed. Handed over to 3rd Lowland Infantry Brigade. Work as usual. | |
| | 22/7/19 | | To Reception Camp. L/Swainston & No.1 Section to PATTSCHEID. Rest of DABRINGHAUSEN for pontooning completed. | |

Army Form C. 2118.

# WAR DIARY
## or
## INTELLIGENCE SUMMARY.

(Erase heading not required.)

Instructions regarding War Diaries and Intelligence Summaries are contained in F. S. Regs., Part II. and the Staff Manual respectively. Title pages will be prepared in manuscript.

| Place | Date | Hour | Summary of Events and Information | Remarks and references to Appendices |
|---|---|---|---|---|
| BURSCHEID, GERMANY. | 23/9/19 | | 19 Pontoons superstructure received from 1st Pontoon Park sent to PATTSCHEID. | |
| | 24/9/19 & 25/9/19 | | No 4 Section H/s WILSON. R.G.A. (attached) to PATTSCHEID. Completion of hut from STUMPF to Demob BURSCHEID. Church Parade. 2 Lt NEWMAN. M.M. R.E. leave to U.K. Work on Camp at PATTSCHEID. 2/Lt NEWMAN. M.M. R.E. nominated for service in EGYPT. 2 Lt A.N. PATRICK. R.E. left for U.K. for transfer to INDIA. 2 Lt R. TURNBULL R.E. leave to U.K. | |
| PATTSCHEID, GERMANY. | 26/9/19 | | Remainder of Company forward proceeded to PATTSCHEID. Lt Lysington R.E. to Hospital. Work on Latrines, Lectures Allusion Bench & making small footways. | |
| | 27/9/19 | | Exploring. Explanation of superstructure. Knocking & erecting superstructure, erecting anchor. Instructor O.C. | |

Army Form C. 2118.

# WAR DIARY
## or
## INTELLIGENCE SUMMARY
*(Erase heading not required.)*

Instructions regarding War Diaries and Intelligence Summaries are contained in F. S. Regs., Part II. and the Staff Manual respectively. Title pages will be prepared in manuscript.

| Place | Date | Hour | Summary of Events and Information | Remarks and references to Appendices |
|---|---|---|---|---|
| PATTSCHEID, GERMANY. | 28/9/19 | | Making rafts, Running Drill, Cooling and weighing anchor. Instructor O.C. | |
| | 29/9/19 | | Making rafts, forming bridge from rafts. Instr. O.C. | |
| | 30/9/19 | | Making rafts, forming bridge & cutts. Instr. O.C. O.C. returned from leave and ordered to report to War Office. Major K.F. Powell D.S.C. R.E. assuming command of Unit R.E. Visited Lamb & Church Parades. | |
| | 31/9/19 | | Nos demobilized during month .. 15 O.R. Nos joined during month .. NIL. | |

[signature]

MAJOR, R.E.
O.C. 497TH (KENT) FIELD CO: R.E.

**CONFIDENTIAL**

# WAR DIARY
## OF
## 497TH FIELD Co. R.E.

### SOUTHERN DIVISION

FROM SEPT 1ST TO SEPT 30TH/'19

Army Form C. 2118.

# WAR DIARY
## or
## INTELLIGENCE SUMMARY.
(Erase heading not required.)

497½ (KENT) FIELD Co. R.E.

| Place | Date | Hour | Summary of Events and Information | Remarks and references to Appendices |
|---|---|---|---|---|
| PATTSCHEID GERMANY. | 1/9/19 | | Loading up Weighing Anchors. Forming up. Lieut: O.C. | |
| | 2/9/19 | | C.R.E. left for ENGLAND. Major A. Russell D.S.O.R.E. assumed command of Coil Rte. Lieut: O.C. | |
| | 3/9/19 | | Forming up. Lieut: O.C. | |
| | 4/9/19 | | Forming up, Cuts, and Breaking up into rafts. Lieut: O.C. | |
| | 5/9/19 | | Welden's needle. 2 needle launched. Lieut: O.C. | |
| | 6/9/19 | | Construction of Welden trestles & high bridge. Lieut: O.C. | |
| | 7/9/19 | | Company bathing. Disinfestation of blankets. | |
| | 8/9/19 | | Church Parade. | |
| | 9/9/19 | | Completion of High Bridge. Rowing Drill. Lieut: O.C. | |
| | 10/9/19 | | Dismantling High Bridge & Welden trestles. Rowing Drill. | |
| | | | Cleaning Shells experimenting. Major A. Russell D.S.O.R.E. ordered to proceed to Engineer Railway Depot BORDEN for duty. | |

Army Form C. 2118.

# WAR DIARY
## or
## INTELLIGENCE SUMMARY.
(Erase heading not required.)

Instructions regarding War Diaries and Intelligence Summaries are contained in F.S. Regs., Part II. and the Staff Manual respectively. Title pages will be prepared in manuscript.

| Place | Date | Hour | Summary of Events and Information | Remarks and references to Appendices |
|---|---|---|---|---|
| PATTSCHEID, GERMANY. | 9.12.19. | | Clearing pontoons & superstructure for return to No 1 Pontoon Park. Lieut. R. Reynell R.E. demobilized in England. 56 O.R. demobilized since last return. Completed "Derby" men who mobilized between 17.9. & 30.9.16. Adjutant returned from leave. Return of Welder sent resubstructure to BURSCHEID. | |
| | 13.9.19 | | Lieut. K.A.K. BARKER-SIMSON R.E. transferred to Company from 510th (Gordon) Field Coy R.E. Company leaving Germany. Major W.Revell D.S.O. R.E. handed over Company to Lieut. K.A.K. BARKER-SIMSON. R.E. | |

Army Form C. 2118.

# WAR DIARY
## or
## INTELLIGENCE SUMMARY.
(Erase heading not required.)

Instructions regarding War Diaries and Intelligence Summaries are contained in F. S. Regs., Part II. and the Staff Manual respectively. Title pages will be prepared in manuscript.

| Place | Date | Hour | Summary of Events and Information | Remarks and references to Appendices |
|---|---|---|---|---|
| PATTSCHEID GERMANY | 12th | | Usual Daily Routine. Average demob. 6 men per diem. | |
| | 13th | | Do. | |
| | 14th | | Do. | |
| | 15th | | Do. | |
| | 16th | | Completion of Final Preparation for return of Pontoons. | |
| | 17th | | All Pontoons and Bridging Equipment returned to No 1 Pontoon Park. | |
| | 18th | | Striking of PATTSCHEID Camp Commenced. | |
| | 19th | | Cleaning up and Clearing Camp Site | |
| | 20th | | Do. | |
| | 21st | | No Work done. LIEUT SWANSTON took ex 36 C.C.S. (sick.) | |
| | 22nd | | PATTSCHEID Camp Broken up. Tentage returned to D.A.D.O.S. Men returned to Coy Hdqrs at BURSCHEID. | |

Army Form C. 2118.

# WAR DIARY
## or
## INTELLIGENCE SUMMARY.
(Erase heading not required.)

Instructions regarding War Diaries and Intelligence Summaries are contained in F. S. Regs., Part II. and the Staff Manual respectively. Title pages will be prepared in manuscript.

| Place | Date | Hour | Summary of Events and Information | Remarks and references to Appendices |
|---|---|---|---|---|
| BURSCHEID GERMANY | 23rd | | Billets in New School cleaned up prepared for evacuation. Coy demobilization completed (less 2 1 in hosp & 2 in U.K. on leave) | |
| | 24th | | do | |
| | 25th | | do | |
| | 26th | | Billets above evacuated. All men of Coy moved into Hutments 2/Cpl Williams (absentee) rejoined from U.K. under escort. | |
| | 27th | | Coy Billets in School handed back to BURGOMEISTER. All leave stopped owing to Railway Strike in U.K. | |
| | 28th | | All movement of tpts by R.K. Stopped for Strikers. Railways in U.K. | |
| | 29th | | Reg¹ Canteen and outbuildings handed back to BURGOMEISTER | |
| | 30th | | Usual routine | |

Kenneth Barker Simcoe
Capt
R.E.
O.C. 497TH (KENT) FIELD CO. R.E.

Secret

War Diary.
from
O.C.
497 Field Company R.E.

Volume No 42.

from 1/10/19 to 27/10/19.

Army Form C. 2118.

# WAR DIARY
## or
## INTELLIGENCE SUMMARY.
*(Erase heading not required.)*

| Place | Date | Hour | Summary of Events and Information | Remarks and references to Appendices |
|---|---|---|---|---|
| BURSCHED GERMANY. | 1/10. | | MAJOR G.J. MARSTON, D.S.O. M.C. R.E. assumed Command of Southern Div? R.E. Coy Routine as usual. | |
| | 2/10. | | Usual Coy Routine. CRE inspected Camp & Horse Lines. | |
| | 3/10. | | Routine as usual. H.Q R.E. Petrol handed to 497 Coy for custody. | |
| | 4/10. | | Dug-out Petrol Store commenced. Convalescency Baths in morning. Combined training for all 3 Coys inaugurated | |
| | 5/10. | | Sunday. Usual Routine | |
| | 6/10. | | Work on Petrol Dug-out continued. | |
| | 7/10. | | Do. Completed. | |
| | 8/10. | | Usual Routine | |
| | 9/10. | | Do | |
| | 10/10. | | 1.O.M. dismissed. Escort sent to A.P.M. BOULOGNE to bring back Sapper RICHARDS, absentee arrested in R.H. | |
| | 11/10. | | Coy Routine as usual | |
| | 12/10. | | do | |
| | 13/10. | | do | |

**Army Form C. 2118.**

# WAR DIARY
## or
## INTELLIGENCE SUMMARY.

(Erase heading not required.)

Instructions regarding War Diaries and Intelligence Summaries are contained in F. S. Regs., Part II. and the Staff Manual respectively. Title pages will be prepared in manuscript.

| Place | Date | Hour | Summary of Events and Information | Remarks and references to Appendices |
|---|---|---|---|---|
| BURSCHEID GERMANY | 14/10 | | Routine as usual. | |
| | 15/10 | | do | |
| | 16/10 | | Spr RICHARDS (Absentee) and escort returned from BOULOGNE | |
| | 17/10 | | Lewis Gunn checks by L.G.O. 52nd Bgn Seven Regr. 16 Miles evacuated | |
| | 18/10 | | Usual Routine | |
| | 19/10 | | Preparations for handing in Stores to D.A.D.O.S. | |
| | 20/10 | | Handed over Company to Major W ? Baines R.E. | |
| | 22/10/19 | | Moved to Mulheim | |

signature

MAJOR R.E.
O.C. 497TH (KENT) FIELD CO: R.E.

www.ingramcontent.com/pod-product-compliance
Lightning Source LLC
Chambersburg PA
CBHW080908230426
43664CB00016B/2753